Trickonometry

To my husband Gary,
both indulgent and irreplaceable!

In memory of my horse, Dial,
the first trickster in my life,
and the "wind beneath my wings."

Trickonometry

The Secrets of Teaching Your Horse Tricks

by Carole Fletcher

Published by
Horse Hollow Press, Inc.
© 2002

Library of Congress Control Number: 2002112446

ISBN: 0-9638814-5-0

FOREWORD

By Carol Harris, owner of Rugged Lark, two-time Super Horse
and two-time Super Horse Sire

Carole Fletcher has a unique talent for teaching horses how
to enjoy tricks. Her ability stems from her wide experience in show
business combined with a rare common sense approach.

We taught Rugged Lark a few tricks because he always showed us
such an eagerness to learn. In doing so, his response to cues and his
willingness to please has only further endeared him to his many friends.

In this one-of-a-kind book, Carole is willing to share her secrets
with loving horse people, hoping to enable them to find other ways
to have fun with their horses.

         — Carol Harris
         Bo-Bett Farm

Author Carole Fletcher and her Paint Stallion, Heza Night Train, performing the Pedestal Pose: Statue of Liberty, see page 64. Photo courtesy of Chris Sartre.

C O N T E N T S

IMPORTANT NOTE

Dear Reader,

Horse Hollow Press is proud to present **Trickonometry: The Secrets of Teaching Your Horse Tricks**. We're sure it will bring you and your horse years of enjoyment and greatly enhance your relationship with your horse!

As with all aspects of horse care and training, teaching your horse tricks requires care, caution, and patience on your part. You should always check with your trainer to make sure a trick is appropriate for you and your horse to learn. Carole Fletcher is an accomplished horsewoman of over 40 years with countless hours of training, education and guidance behind her. While having fun with her horses, she does demand discipline and the most exemplary manners. Realistically assess your own skills and your horse's training level and ability before attempting any of these tricks, and, if possible, work with your trainer to help you teach them. Importantly, follow the sequence of tricks outlined by the author in the Table of Contents and the Introduction. There is a reason to her order that directly relates to your horse's learning. And, finally, always remember to use appropriate protective gear for you and your horse.

With these recommendations in mind, it is our pleasure to share with you these fabulous, easy-to-teach tricks! Have fun teaching and performing the tricks within this book.

—Horse Hollow Press

Photo courtesy of Chris Sartre

C arole Fletcher is one of the best known trick horse trainers in the United States. She has trained, performed and offered clinics with trick horses since 1976, often before audiences of thousands at state fairs, festivals, resorts, theme parks, leading equestrian events, schools, camps, parades, advertising promos and TV commercials. She is the creator of the program Trick Horse™ Training.

A horse enthusiast her entire life, she has competed at the Paint Nationals, World Championship, Quarter Horse Congress, and Pinto Nationals, earning numerous national and regional level awards and championships.

Carole has been featured on national television on NBC, ABC and on WMUR-TV. Articles about her have appeared in *Horse & Rider, Paint Horse Journal, Horse Illustrated, Palomino Horse Journal* and the *Horsemen's Yankee Pedlar*. She is also widely known for her articles on Trick Horse™ Training, which have appeared in more than 35 publications across the country, as well as a dozen internet sites. She has six videos on trick horse training.

Carole did doctoral degree work at Rutgers University, received her M.A. degree in Education from Hunter College and her B.A. degree in Education from Fairleigh Dickinson University. Her teaching experience has enabled her to share her knowledge with others. She operates Singin' Saddles Ranch in Reddick, Florida and can be reached via her website at www.trickhorse.com.

Carole and Dial "sitting down on the job!" Photo courtesy of Chris Sartre

PREFACE

Some people don't take trick training seriously, perhaps because both horse and handler seem to enjoy performing tricks so much, or tricks seem less important than other behaviors. However, any behavior we teach our horses, even tricks, will involve the learning process, and can result in on-cue behaviors which the horse performs reliably. Why shouldn't the learning process be fun for both horse and handler? Horses of all breeds, ages and disciplines can easily be taught tricks, but let's restore some dignity to these "trick" behaviors that require as much effective communication as do other behaviors.

Most horse owners want to teach their horse a few tricks. Until now the process required a lot of trial-and-error attempts, too much ingenuity and a great deal of horse-training knowledge, all of which inevitably led to major frustration. One fellow who attended my clinic told me it had taken two years to teach his horse to "sit up," since all he knew to do was to wait for the horse to get up from lying down into a sitting position and be quick to treat him. He was hoping the horse would lie down often!

There are few books or videos on the subject of trick-training horses. Most performers and trainers of performing horses, such as those in the circuses or movie and entertainment industries, in my opinion, are reluctant to reveal their methods, unless you are working with them as assistants or family members. If you wanted to teach a horse tricks, much was left for someone to figure out for himself.

I am sure most people have met a few horses that they thought were veritable geniuses—who amazed them by performing a trick, maybe even two. The horses' owners loved owning the smartest horse in the barn! People want to believe they've met a wonder horse, not just a horse that has been cleverly trained.

One question I am frequently asked about my star pupil, Night Train, is whether he was born a genius, since he has such a large—over fifty—repertoire of tricks and high school movements. He is hardly the smartest horse that ever existed, but he might just be the one that has acquired the greatest amount of skills. What seems to be human-like intelligence was actually taught.

So why should you put all this time into teaching tricks when you hardly have time to ride your horse?

First, you will see marvelous changes in the horse you love. He will get brighter, more interesting and shine with intelligence. You will learn to communicate with him on a finer and higher level, and he will learn to listen and to communicate with you. You, not only he, will get attention and praise. Inside you, there's a ham waiting to break into "show biz." With your trick horse as your sidekick, you can do it. You can entertain in your barn or on "stage." How far you take it is entirely up to you.

You can begin trick training and make him a comedian, a helper, a playmate for your kids. He can earn you respect or earn you money. He can learn to say his "prayers," and take a "nap." He can shake hands and give you a hoof. He can give you a good laugh. He can give you more pleasure than ever before and have a whale of a good time doing it.

In just a month or two of working with this book you'll find that you will have acquired a lot of horse-training knowledge. You might consider putting your own imagination to work on possible tricks that are not covered in this book. I think you'll have a lot of fun with it.

I really enjoy teaching my horses tricks. I receive more positive feedback from my horses and from the people who see them than from any other thing I do. I am sure you will find teaching the tricks in this book an enjoyable way to further the education of your horse, while leaving him panting for more. But the best part, by far, is that these tricks enable your horse to unleash his animal magnetism on everyone he meets!

Whoever that furry creature in the barn is reading over your shoulder, I wish you and him good luck and hope you both enjoy your new knowledge and newly acquired tricks and talents.

Carole Fletcher
Singin' Saddles Ranch, Florida

INTRODUCTION

Let Me Entertain You

Let us first examine the origin of trick horses. Horses have long been used for the purpose of entertaining people. The Greeks and Romans depended heavily on trick horses in their equestrian spectacles for the popular appeal of their public games and entertainments. The circus, as we know it today, had its beginnings with the itinerant performer who gave equestrian performances, demonstrating his skills of horsemanship in medieval village marketplaces. Schools of classical horsemanship, such as the Spanish Riding School, developed training methods used by circuses for their performing horses, who later became known as Trick Horses. Down through the ages came the thundering hooves of horses as they performed for mankind, thrilling thousands at circuses and Wild West Shows. Advertised as the "World's Most Beautiful Horses, The Pride of the Tented World," trick horses enchanted the public as they displayed their clever and breathtaking poses and feats.

With the advent of the cinema came the movie hero cowboy and his horse. Along came stars such as Gene Autry and Champion, and Roy Rogers and Trigger, who was billed as the "World's Smartest Horse." These famous horses displayed many heroic and spectacular tricks, movements and gestures as their masters cued them with commands and signals. These clean-cut cowboys and their equine partners became children's heroes, and were toted to school on lunch boxes and toys. Their names were household words. The cowboy heroes of yesteryear have given way to Star Wars characters, karate kids, and Batman as icons. However, talented performing horses still have their place in circuses, fairs, movies and commercials, and there would be a void without them.

During the last four decades, the numbers of horses in the United States have increased to a present population of approximately seven million, and the numbers of Americans involved as horse owners, service providers and employees are slightly greater, at 7.1 million. The prosperous American economy has enabled people to own horses for many uses: pleasure, recreation, racing, driving and show. Those who are involved in showing horses in a variety of riding and driving disciplines will have to agree that the trick horse differs from the show or competition horse. The show horse demonstrating his abilities is criticized by one or several judges. The trick horse may be criticized by thousands of people. There are many trainers for show horses. There are few trainers for the performing trick horse.

I have had the benefit of being able to observe several trick trainers go through their training techniques. I have utilized what I feel are the most gentle, humane methods on my animals. They are a joy to watch perform because they are alert and happy in the job they are doing. This book was written so that you and your horses may benefit from my years of training knowledge and experience, and share the same kind of partnership that I have with my animals.

Establishing a Relationship with Your Horse

My relationship with horses I have owned has always been one of companionship and friendship. I trained my show horses slowly and methodically, gaining their love and trust by asking them to understand what it was I wanted them to do, not forcing them, and rewarding them for appropriate behavior. Petite woman that I am, forcing a horse that is ten or twelve times my weight would have been most difficult anyway. Since I have

also taught children, I applied my formula for teaching children to teaching horses: love, kindness and understanding.

I have observed fear and resignation on the faces of many horses, many of whom are show horses who act and move like mechanical robots. Any animal can be taught by fear, but fear will generally produce a dangerous, nervous animal and one that cannot be trusted. Any animal should know that must respect and mind you, and if you use kindness and understanding in your lessons, he will accept whatever discipline is necessary and return it in kind to you.

Success in horse training comes from effective communication. You undoubtedly know that effective communication is hard enough with people, let alone with horses! But bear in mind that your pal Skipper just wants to please you. He's usually happy to accommodate your requests if he understands what it is you want him to do. Being aware of whether your horse is getting your message or not will help you to understand your horse better and will also allow you to be more effective in trying to communicate with him. If he isn't getting the message, ask yourself why. You will discover it is almost always something you are doing wrong.

Many fine horsemen are observers of horse behavior and truly understand the "language" of the horse. They assess the interaction between horses, herd dynamics, which gives them a clue about their relationship with a horse. Spend some time watching your horse out in his paddock alone and with other horses, and you will be surprised at his responses and behaviors. Observing horse behavior gives a horseman insight into the horse's mind. An expert horseman has the ability to "read" a horse, that is, think like one, and to act accordingly.

I spend a considerable amount of time observing my horses, in their stalls, pastures, at rest, work and play. I firmly believe that they can think and reason. I watched Dial figure out how to open up his door by playing with the latch, and then proceed to open up his buddies' doors to let them out, too. If he liked the greener grass on the other side of the fence, he'd jump it (if it wasn't high enough). I swear that Dial had measured the height of the fences and calculated the exact distances needed to jump them.

Photo courtesy of Michelle Younghans

At my training barn, I gave lessons to students, all of whom were accustomed to giving their school horse a carrot after the lesson. My trick horse, Night Train, came to recognize this procedure, and since he was trained with treats and rewards, he would start entertaining or amusing the students by doing anything to get their attention—all for the carrot, of course. Usually he would flap his upper lip or smile at them. The result? They brought an extra carrot for him! He had figured out that he had to do something "cute" so that he'd get a treat, too.

Think horses don't reason? Think again!

Since I perform publicly and film commercials, my horses have many distracting things to contend with: noise, banners, smoke, light effects, unusual odors (such as elephants and camels), firecrackers, water obstacles and wind. If I didn't have a horse that trusted me unconditionally, there might have been some serious wrecks in potentially dangerous situations, some of them without any barriers between my horse and the crowds.

One TV commercial was filmed inside a bar and dancehall saloon with blasting music and strobe lights. Another was filmed on a windy night, in the dark, with smoke and lightning effects, shot at the end of a rocky cliff, while he reared (resembling a wild stallion) at liberty with nothing more than a rope enclosure around him. Had I not had Night Train's complete trust in me that no harm would come to him, serious accidents might have occurred. This kind of trust is precious and takes a long time to cultivate, but worth every minute doing so.

17

How the Horse Learns Tricks

Many of the movements or tricks we are going to ask the horse to do he already knows how to do without commands from the trainer or performer. He knows how to shake his head, curl his upper lip, sit up, kneel and lie down. He has done all of these and many others on his own. Now we are going to ask him to do them on cue or command. But first we should know something about how the horse learns in general.

The horse learns in very much the same way as a child. He has a short attention span, but an excellent memory. Once you teach a horse a trick, he will never forget the cues for it. As long as he is physically able to do it, he will.

The principles of conditioning, shaping and positive reinforcement can be applied to teaching horses tricks or high school movements. Many of the natural horsemanship trainers (or "horse whisperers") recommend building a horse's confidence through trust and reward rather than fear and intimidation. Conditioning refers to the repeated association of a certain cue with a behavior, until that

Photo courtesy of Michelle Younghans

cue causes the behavior. For example, if you tug slightly down on a lead rope when leading a horse and stop walking, simultaneously commanding him to "whoa," then sooner of later he will also stop walking. If he stops walking, then you stop tugging on the lead rope (releasing the pressure of the halter and lead rope), and in doing so you are using negative reinforcement (moving away from discomfort) to reinforce his stopping.

Now if we decide instead to use positive reinforcers for correct behavior, we need to think of things that are really pleasurable for him: praise, a good pat (not slap!), or some food reward or tidbit he likes. I suggest you get to know what pleases your horse, then try to vary the rewards among those favorites. In trick-training I lean toward using food rewards and occasionally mix in others. I find this method the most effective and time efficient. At the end of a training session, a good reward is to be "put away."

I have discovered that the most successful practice of using food rewards with my trick horses is established by decreasing the amount of treats once the trick is learned.

When I am shaping behavior, however — that is, teaching it in small steps — I generously reward them with treats.

You have already established control over your horse with basic ground manners and handling, such as leading, stopping, stall and pasture manners, standing quietly for grooming, having his hooves picked up and trimmed, tying and perhaps longeing. If not, you should have all of these as a solid foundation, and then proceed to teach tricks. When your horse respects your space and is completely at ease in handling, then bring on the tricks!

The enthusiasm you build with food rewards is very important for performing tricks. An unhappy or indifferent horse will give a lackluster performance. The more your horse injects extra brilliance and enthusiasm into his work, the better it is for your "act." The smallest of treats works the best to keep your horse motivated and happy. I usually use 2 inch pieces of carrots, which I carry in my pockets, an apron or a fanny pack. A small piece of carrot is enough to be eaten quickly so that you can get right back to the training. Your horse will consider it a welcome reward. I don't like to use sugar because I think it has a tendency to make a horse mean. Some horses who have never been fed a carrot before may need to get used to them as treats before starting trick work.

Whatever the reward, it should be given immediately so that the horse associates the reward with the particular action that pleased you. Many horse trainers advocate a 3-second rule for reward or discipline with a horse. Your timing should be quick enough so that you are very clear about rewarding the desired behavior, within 3 seconds of that behavior, or exactly when that behavior occurs. If you follow the 3-second rule, the horse can clearly know what he was doing and repeat it again for another reward. Delays between trick behavior and reward can lead to confusion. Timing is everything!

Some people might think that using food rewards can create problems for horse training. You must be careful not to reward the horse for bad behavior, such as nipping, biting, or trying to mug you or nose-dive into your pockets for treats. Some horses can get greedy. Only reward your horse when he does the trick behavior. He will begin to move away from your pockets as time passes. With some horses, this can mean a few minutes and with others a few days.

How do you start teaching a trick to your horse? This book reveals the small, simple steps you should follow in teaching each trick. Alternative approaches to teaching particular tricks will also be offered. A trick that appears complex and impossible to teach even to the smartest horse is successful for that reason alone. All the seemingly difficult tricks can easily be taught to any horse.

We're going to use a process called shaping to teach each trick. Put simply, the horse will offer you a likeness of the gesture or movement you ask for. Reward if the likeness is what you want. Ignore the response if it is not what you have asked for and then ask again for the desired gesture. Sooner or later your horse will respond by giving you a likeness that pleases you, and then you must be prompt to reward. When offering a smile, for example, he may curl his upper lip up just slightly. You must be quick to reward even the slightest upper lip movement. Eventually the horse will turn his upper lip up all the way and hold it there. This is how the horse learns. You provide cues, he makes a response in the right way and then you reward.

Attention, Please!

If you are going to teach a horse anything, first you must have his attention, whether dismounted or mounted. This means the horse must listen to you and watch you with both his eyes and ears. **It bears repeating here: before attempting tricks, your horse should be solid in basic groundwork and handling, respectful and obedient. If this good foundation is laid out, then it makes the new challenge of teaching him tricks much easier.**

No one can teach the horse anything if his attention is not on you, the handler, and if he is looking at things and constantly moving around. You should have the horse's attention as he stands quietly next to you. Standing quietly means standing still and relaxed. A still but tense horse will not remember what you are asking.

The horse's attention span will be short in the beginning stages of learning, but will gradually become longer as he is being trained, both on the ground and from the saddle. It helps to begin training a horse in a place that is free from distractions, so that he can focus on the trainer. This gives your horse the best opportunity to learn. It would be hard for him to pay attention to you if he is bothered by other horses and things going on. I prefer to start teaching a horse tricks in a stall for this reason, or some other quiet place out of sight and sound of his pasture mates. There, he should be relaxed and focused. If the horse is excited,

you should be patient and try calming the horse with a soft voice and stroking him on the neck with your hand.

After a trick is mastered, practice it in different locations and with different distractions. You want your horse to perform regardless of life's noises, unfamiliar odors, and the presence of other animals or young children.

To maintain consistency and keep from confusing the horse, it is best to have only one trick trainer work in the barn. However, once a trick is completely mastered, it can be demonstrated by anyone. You should require the person to know the commands and cues, and to attain a certain level of performance from your horse before rewarding him. You don't want your training reversed.

Your patience will be tried when teaching your horse tricks. Although most horses are willing, in the beginning stages, they may not understand what you want them to do. You need to get the horse's confidence and let him know you will not hurt him. You will get his respect and obedience, but not make him fear you or get excited. An excitable, nervous horse cannot learn. He must be relaxed in order to learn and remember.

Gear the length of your training sessions to your horse's attention span. Short sessions in training that are repeated frequently produce fast results. Teach him a lesson for fifteen minutes or so, then put him away and repeat it an hour or so later. At least two sessions a day are preferred, one in the morning and the same later in the day. Allow your horse to succeed throughout each session and be sure to end it on a high note. If your horse falters on a particular step of a trick you are teaching, you are probably proceeding too fast. Go back to where you can end the training on a positive note and move on to something else. In your next session, back up a little in your training and rebuild your horse's confidence. It may take you 10-12 more fifteen-minute training sessions to teach a trick. But for less than three hours of training, your horse will look as if he's ready to apply for a scholarship to your local university!

To avoid monotony for yourself and your horse, work on the different elements of a particular trick or on several different tricks during the same training session. Try to make a little progress with each element and move on to the next. Wrap up the training session at the slightest sign that your horse is tiring. You'll see terrific progress if you follow these suggestions! Through-out your train-

Photo courtesy of Michelle Younghans

ing sessions, keep a constant flow of positive feedback to your horse. Like people, horses that are complimented for a job well-done, rather than condemned for a few mistakes along the way, will progress faster and more happily. You will need to remind yourself of this often!

Okay...Now on Cue!

We use the same aids in teaching a trick or high school horse as we use on any other horse in training: natural and artificial aids. The natural aids are your body weight, hands and legs. The artificial aids consist of the whip, spurs and the voice. You may need equipment in teaching certain tricks, such as a long whip, a saddle or surcingle, and a long soft cotton lead rope. A longe line and longe whip will come in handy as well.

Most of the horse's cues will be signals from your body position (where you are standing if dismounted, or your seat if mounted), hands, feet or legs and voice. You will ask the horse with the aids to do a trick, he makes some sort of response, then you reward him. Your cues will always be the same, with or without a whip. It is most important that you try to stick to the exact words and hand/whip signals I recommend. Your horse will learn 27 new word commands if you teach him every trick in this book. Consistency in using the same words, the same logical word order, and the same method of speaking is necessary for clear communication. The hand/whip cues and body positions used are each unique from the horse's point of view. You have to trust me on my selections. Space limitations preclude an in-depth explanation of why certain words or cues are used.

As you pick the tricks you'd like to work on, remember to keep variety in mind. Don't pick three "picking up things with the mouth" tricks to do back-to-back in your performance. Instead, alternate them with non-picking up tricks. Your audience will never notice any similarities and it will make for a better show. Feel free to use any of my humor from the book during a performance. Chances are you will come up with other humorous lines for your situation. You want to loosen up your audience. They will enjoy the performance more. Also, you'll want to reduce distractions before a performance.

Once you have taught a trick, you might consider putting your own imagination to work on how you can present it, or work on possible tricks that are not covered in this book. Let your imagination and creativity soar!

Photo courtesy of Michelle Younghans

Suggested Sequence of Training

If you are this far along in the introduction, chances are you're serious about teaching your horse tricks. Just like there are ABCs a child must learn in grade school before going on to middle, junior and high school, the same principle applies to trick-training. Like a child, the horse learns by learning, and enjoys the rewards he gets for "right" answers, attention, praise and showing off. Your children learn addition in school before proceeding to learn geometry, right? Why would we ask any more of the horse? And yet, there are people who always ask me if they can teach their horses to lie down or rear first, because they think that those tricks are most impressive.

In the first place, you never want to teach a horse a trick that might be potentially dangerous to both horse and handler. If you taught your horse to rear early on in his trick work, chances are he would try to please you and constantly rear—NOT a good idea! You want to teach him first some innocuous trick, such as smiling, so it won't present you or others with safety problems in handling him. Moreover, tricks such as rearing and lying down require some physical exertion for which your horse may not be conditioned. In addition, tricks such as lying down and bowing place the horse in a vulnerable position from which he cannot escape. I don't think his trust or confidence is built up enough yet at the beginning stage of his trick education. Sure, they may be flashy tricks, but will they do more harm than good to you and to your horse?

I have found that I am most successful by teaching simple tricks first. These tricks do not require any real agility or props. Rather, I am establishing a bond or relationship with the horse, based on companionship, trust, patience and reward. The ABCs I refer to are my tone of voice, body position, and use of the whip, all while centered around teaching him tricks with his head, neck and mouth. I introduce the various articles he will be handling with his mouth. I also teach him to stand still, or to walk away from me and return if I am going to work him at liberty (without halter, lead rope or bridle).

The tricks I recommend teaching using the horse's head in the beginning are: **Kiss, Put Your Head on My Shoulder, Acting "Ashamed," Answering Questions "Yes" and "No,"** and **Pushing You Around**.

The easy tricks I start with to teach him to use his mouth and neck are: **Smile, Taking a Hanky From Your Pocket, Taking a Hat Off Your Head And Give It to You, Waving a Flag** and **Drinking From a Bottle**. These tricks are easy for the horse to learn and easy for you to teach. You are establishing up to this point confidence and obedience, and the use of the whip in his early training without scaring him at all. If you tried to start the horse out with more difficult tricks, he would not be mentally ready. I find that by waiting to have learned this much, the horse will be concerned and surprised, not mad and scared, when you tap him with the whip around his legs for the succeeding tricks.

The next series of tricks using the horse's legs and feet are: **Shaking Hands, Counting, Stretching, Crossing Legs, Bowing, Kneeling, Lying Down** and **Sitting Up**. I put these lessons in this particular sequence for good reason: The horse becomes accustomed to my handling his legs and feet, and my pointing at him to cue him with the whip. He is also learning to position his body by certain pressures, and by now has become quite familiar with my tone of voice, touch and manner of speaking. He is also learning to give me his undivided attention or else the whip might "remind" him. Still up to this point, all of his movements are natural, ones that he does on his own (without cues). All of these are necessary as prior schooling to asking your horse to do movements and pose in unnatural positions with or without equipment.

By the time you have taught these preceding tricks, you and your horse will be ready for a more difficult series: **Curtsy Bow, Statue Of Liberty Pose** and **End Of The Trail Pose**.

In this series, your horse will learn to acquire his balance on a pedestal. If he should fall or overturn a piece of equipment at this point, it is likely that he will be less apt to be afraid, since he knows he can trust you not to put him in a dangerous situation.

The recommended sequence of training I've outlined is not cemented in stone. You may want to alter it to suit your needs. I have found it has worked for me and my horses and so pass it on to you.

Recognize your horse's natural abilities and capitalize on those talents. The next section will show you how your horse's personality fits into the scheme of trick training.

Choosing a Horse for Trick Training

So, you have a smart, beautiful animal and you would like to teach him a few tricks. If this is the first horse you are starting to trick-train, just remember that your first horse will be a "guinea pig," and is going to be the one you are going to make many mistakes on in training. You need the practice work and need a horse to practice with. You may make a pretty good trick horse out of your first one, but every succeeding horse you practice on is going to turn out better that the first horse you work with.

People always ask me if the sex of a trick horse matters. To this question my response is that it depends on what you plan on doing with a trick horse. If you plan on teaching a mare tricks for your own challenge and amusement, I would say fine. However, if you plan on performing with a mare whose performance will be affected by heat cycles (seems she's always in heat for a show), then a gelding or stallion (providing you are capable of handling one) will be more reliable.

You can start trick-training a weanling, but remember my previous advice about having a solid foundation in manners and ground training. Besides this necessary foundation, like children, young horses just don't have the attention span of an older horse, and it is only while you have his attention that he will learn.

If you plan on doing exhibitions with the horse, consider his age so that you get enough useful years of productivity out of him. An older horse, too, may have physical limitations that a younger horse does not have. I would venture to say that the trick horse has a longer life span than most other working horses. A testimonial to this statement is that my exhibition trick horse Dial still performed up until his last months (at our facility, not "on the road"), and died at 32 years old. In fact, when he saw the trailer hitched up, he always ran to the gate, even towards the end, thinking there was a show somewhere he was going to.

The size of the horse is a consideration depending on where you want to perform, and the equipment you will need. Obviously, you will need a larger pedestal for a draft horse than you would for a mini. I have had to perform indoors and bring horses through doors, on elevators, on slippery wooden floors, and on concrete floors, pavement and up stairs. I have performed with all sizes of horses from drafts to minis. In fact, I usually capitalized on the size of the horse in my acts. A big draft horse just begs for comic humor, and so does a mini. I even had a draft and mini together, sort of a Mutt and Jeff routine—what a hoot that act was!

Pick a horse that is sound, a good mover, relaxed and supple. He should have good vision and hearing. Make certain that physically he is capable of doing the movements you ask of him. Don't expect a Mack truck to perform like a sports car!

Although you can dress up a horse in costumes, a horse that is easy to remember (that is, one that is of unusual color) is one that will stand out. At any rate, the trick horse should be one that is pleasing to look at.

Now here comes the really important factor in your selection—the horse's disposition and temperament. Disposition, or his willingness to work, may be changed to some extent by you. A horse's temperament, however, is inherited and cannot be altered. An excitable, nervous horse is much slower to learn since he does not want to conform to training easily, whereas others are more inclined to accept training calmly. A horse does not learn when he is nervous and excited. A horse suitable for trick-training should also be one that is at home in practically any surroundings, especially if you plan on taking this horse out to public places to perform. While any horse can learn tricks, some horses, just like people, make the task of teaching them easier than others.

Photo courtesy of Michelle Younghans

Your Horse's Personality

Showing off our horses to the world is far more fun than anyone can imagine. We can show them off for their good looks, for their charm and cuteness, and for their talent and skills. This book will show you how to enhance your horse's instinctive behaviors, and possibly even make him famous by performing new and attention-getting tricks. The fame may only reach as far as your barn, or it may take you all the way to stardom, but either way, it will take your horse deep into your heart.

Most horses will be able to learn all of the tricks in this book. By using the EQUINE PERSONALITY TEST that follows, you will see which tricks are best suited for your individual horse, and which ones will be easiest for your horse to learn. This is your own recipe for a built-in success formula.

If you have more than one horse or know more than one horse, you already know that each horse has its own unique personality. One horse loves to be groomed and the other doesn't, one likes to jump while another hates it, one will run from strange objects and the other will stand and look at them. What makes them different?

Every horse, yours included, is born with a partially pre-determined personality consisting of disposition and temperament. The good trainer will ascertain the horse's qualities and figure out how to work with them.

No doubt your horse's experiences since birth have helped mold his personality. The experiences your horse has had during the critical periods of development have influenced how your horse "sees" the world and reacts to it. But your horse's way of reacting to the world is instinctive, and these instinctive behaviors make up his "personality." These instincts can be seen as natural talents because our horses come programmed with them. They can be broken into three categories: Prey Instinct, Herd Instinct and Flight Instinct. It is the concentration of each instinct that makes up each horse's personality.

You can take a test and actually determine how a horse will react to the surrounding environment. This will tell you what your horse's Instincts are and will give you insight into his personality characteristics. This will help you to understand how your horse learns, and to know which tricks or exercises will be easier to accomplish and which may take a little longer to learn, based solely on your horse's Instincts and Personality Profile. This applies to all of your horse's training, whether mounted or dismounted.

Personality Test

Let's see how your horse's personality is arranged. Each category in this test has a series of questions. If you want to recognize your horse's capabilities, you will need to answer each question honestly.

Answer according to what your horse would do presented by the situation proposed in the question. Points are neither bad nor good. The total score simply gives you the concentration of the three Instincts your horse possesses. With few exceptions, horses will have some of each Instinct. They need all the Instincts to survive in nature.

Prey Instinct behaviors are associated with getting food when horses lived in the wild. They are based on instincts to graze, feed and seek food. Herd Instincts are based on social interaction with both humans and other animals. They show your horse's willingness to be part of a herd that includes you. Flight Instincts refer to your horse's defending with courage his territory or space; in other words, his concern for his well-being. It has to do with how your horse reacts in stressful situations, and his feelings of insecurity and vulnerability; in short, his instincts of self-preservation.

While taking this test for your horse, answer according to what your horse would do if presented with the situation described in each question. If your horse would almost always react this way, score 10 points; for sometimes, score 5 points; or if you believe your horse would hardly ever do what the question says, score 0 points. The total score will simply give you the proportions of the three Instincts that your horse possesses.

Equine Personality Test

Mark your score in the blank after each question. Use 10 for ALWAYS, 5 for SOMETIMES and 0 for HARDLY EVER

BEHAVIOR QUESTIONS

■ PREY INSTINCT

Does your horse:

1. Paw or sniff the ground a lot? _____
2. Get excited by moving objects such as bicycles or squirrels? _____
3. Stalk things or other animals in the grass? _____
4. Bend on one knee to grab some grass under the fence? _____
5. Like to play with or carry things in his mouth? _____
6. Wolf down his food? _____
7. Whinny in a high-pitched voice when excited? _____
8. Nicker when you come to feed him? _____
9. Chase other horses/dogs/animals away from his food? _____
10. Keep his ears pricked forward a lot? _____

Total for Prey Instincts: _____

■ HERD INSTINCT

Does your horse:

1. Get along with other horses? _____
2. Get along with other people? _____
3. Whinny when left alone? _____
4. Stand close to other horses? _____
5. Groom other horses or be groomed by them? _____
6. Follow you around like a shadow? _____
7. Play a lot with other horses? _____
8. Run up to you or other people? _____
9. Keep his ears forward when approached by other horses? _____
10. Show reproductive behaviors, such as mounting or winking? _____

Total for Herd Instinct: _____

■ FLIGHT INSTINCT

Does your horse:

1. Run away from strange objects or sounds? _____
2. Act fearful in unfamiliar situations? _____
3. Have trouble standing still when being groomed? _____
4. Dislike being groomed or bathed? _____
5. Dislike being petted? _____
6. Act nervous when reprimanded? _____
7. Spook at something new that wasn't there before? _____
8. Submit to other horses? _____
9. Run away from new situations? _____
10. Show fear in his eyes at new objects or loud noises? _____

Total for Flight Instinct: _____ ➡

As you can see by the questions themselves, each category tells a little about your horse's psychological makeup. *With few exceptions, horses will have some of each Instinct.* They need all of the Instincts to survive in nature. Even though we now provide their food, they still need Prey Instinct to graze and feed. They need Herd Instinct to live in harmony with us. We secure their safety, but they need Flight Instinct to be able to cope with pressures, like learning new things. How we react to a horse with a lot of Flight Instinct can make or break that horse. A horse with high Flight Instinct can be easily stressed and might live in constant turmoil if not provided with a consistent and stable environment.

The level of each Instinct is what helps you to see into your horse's personality. Any number above 50 is considered high. Obviously, the closer to 100, the higher the Instinct. A horse can be high in all Instincts: Prey, Herd, and Flight, or a horse can be high in only one, or in none. Lower than 30 is considered low in any Instinct.

Being low in an Instinct is not necessarily bad. Being high is not necessarily good.

The numbers are simply teaching you about your horse. True, some Instincts are more desirable for certain tasks. High Prey Instinct will make teaching for treats easier, since your horse will be strongly motivated for a food reward. High Herd Instinct will be desirable for a family horse, or one that will enjoy being around people.

As previously mentioned, high is over 50 and too much of a good thing may not be so desirable either. A high Flight Instinct horse may not be able to concentrate on the task at hand if birds are flying or trees are rustling. *Learn about your horse* so you can be prepared for any situation that you are putting your horse into. Know what to expect from your horse so you won't be surprised or disappointed when your horse acts in a certain way. *Learn to anticipate* how your horse will react by knowing your horse's Personality Profile.

Knowing how to bring out the Instincts in your horse, or knowing what not to do to keep from eliciting certain Instincts in your horse, will help you to communicate better with your horse. You will be using these skills while teaching anything to your horse.

Horses are most *happy* in the Instincts that are *high* for them. Horses are *uncomfortable* if they are in an Instinct that is *low* for them. For some tasks your horse will need to have certain Instincts. If your horse is high in Herd Instinct, give him lots of pats. If he is high in Prey Instinct, offer lots of food treats. You will need to use your imagination and understanding of the Instincts in order to teach him. Practice and learn. Your imagination is your only limitation.

CHAPTER 1

That's Using Your Head

Thise first few simple, fun tricks require no elaborate equipment, and are essentially taught with patience, companionship and reward. Your horse will begin to learn that the cues are from your body position (where you stand), body movements and voice commands. Spend as much time as you think necessary in teaching these first few tricks. Be patient, go slow, don't hurry, especially in the beginning, when he is just starting. Follow these steps in order and be consistent in using the EXACT positions, movements and commands presented here. Your horse will learn each trick faster, as soon as he figures out he'll get goodies for the right answers. Then, you'll see "light bulbs" go off as he's learning! I recommend at least two training sessions every day, at about the same times. Remember horses are creatures of habit.

THE KISS: "Gimme a little kiss, will ya, huh?"

Equipment needed: halter, lead rope, carrots.

He won't kiss and tell!

Photo courtesy of Chris Sartre

STEP 1: Have a halter and lead rope on your horse, standing him in a stall, aisle or next to a fence. Stand directly in front of him. Hold a piece of carrot in your right hand. Let your horse know it is there, but don't give it to him. Place the carrot firmly next to your cheek and let him smell it. He knows it's there, and will probably attempt to get it by reaching closer to your cheek for it. Command, "KISS ME!" while slightly raising your head. As soon as his mouth touches your hand or cheek, give him the carrot.

STEP 2: Repeat Step 1 several times, giving the command each time and continuing the suggestive movement of your head. Reward him with the carrot each time.

STEP 3: Stand in front of your horse, raise your hand slightly, without the carrot and command, "KISS ME!" When your horse raises his mouth and nuzzles your cheek or mouth, pet him, praise him generously and give him a carrot. Repeat this process until your horse thoroughly understands the trick and responds quickly. Do not continue until he tires of it (and he will). You will be able to eliminate the hand gesture eventually and just raise your chin and give him the command. Now he'll give you a sloppy horse kiss whenever you ask for one! But he won't kiss and tell!

Note: You have developed the first "body" cue by standing in front of your horse and raising your head, together with the first verbal "trick" command. You can also use the same steps above to teach the horse to kiss you on the lips. However, be aware, that he may bite you by accident and that this is pretty risky.

PUT YOUR HEAD ON MY SHOULDER: "Hug me, please!"

Equipment needed: halter, lead rope, carrots.

Together, forever!
Photo courtesy of Michelle Younghans

Let's go teach Romeo how to be even more romantic. Now that he knows how to kiss you, he should learn how to put his head on your shoulder, maybe even whisper sweet nothings in your ear! You can put on a little mood music for this one, if you like!

STEP 1: Review the previous lesson and be sure your horse completely understands and performs it correctly, rewarding him when he does it correctly.

STEP 2: With a halter and lead rope on your horse, stand him in a stall, aisle, or next to a fence. Be sure not to tie him to anything, since he needs the freedom of moving his head. Stand slightly in front of his left foreleg, facing the same direction as him and command: "PUT YOUR HEAD ON MY SHOULDER!," emphasizing the word shoulder. Remember — your horse is also developing an extensive vocabulary with these new tricks and responding as well to the tone of your voice.

STEP 3: Take a step closer to him, and with the end of the lead rope in your left hand and the snap part in your right hand, gently pull his head and place it on your right shoulder. As he relaxes and lets it rest there, reward him with a small piece of carrot.

STEP 4: Remove his head with your right hand from your shoulder while simultaneously taking a step forward. Reward him with a small piece of carrot again.

STEP 5: Repeat Steps 2, 3 and 4 until he responds to the combination of your voice command, together with your step backwards. Be sure to reward your horse with a small piece of carrot and praise. You will most likely find he likes resting his head on your shoulder.

STEP 6: Now alternate your cues for "KISS" and "PUT YOUR HEAD ON MY SHOULDER." He should master the differences in your body position, hand movements and voice commands for these two tricks.

Note: You can develop a hug as an extension of the trick and command, "HUG ME!" You will want to hold the carrot out towards your left shoulder so that he has to reach for it to look like he's wrapping his head around you. What makes horse training interesting is that sometimes horses will show you their own individual style, some movement that may not have been in your program. If you like it, you can reward it and incorporate it into his training. If you are open-minded, you can learn a lot from your horse!

How embarrasing!

Photo courtesy of Gary Fletcher

ACTING ASHAMED

Equipment needed: halter, lead rope, carrots.

While your horse's attention is centered around using his head, let us continue to teach him some others using his head (and neck).

STEP 1: Have a halter and lead rope on your horse, standing him in a stall, aisle or next to a fence. Rehearse the first two tricks, KISS, and PUT YOUR HEAD ON MY SHOULDER to refresh his memory. Demand he do them correctly and be sure to reward him when he does. Stand directly in front of him, and with a piece of carrot in your left hand, reach behind your back and under your right arm, turning your body slightly so he can see it. At the same time, raise your right arm level with your shoulder and in a scolding tone of voice, say, "SHAME ON YOU!" Emphasize the word shame.

STEP 2: Make him lower his head, reaching under your right arm for the carrot. You can encourage him by gently pushing his head down with your right hand on his poll, if necessary. Let him eat the carrot, and while doing so, drop your right arm around his head, pet him and reassure him he is good, in a soothing tone of voice. Repeat this several times in one session, say, over a five to ten minute period, but no longer, so that he doesn't tire of it.

STEP 3: Repeat Steps 1 and 2, until your horse immediately drops his head under your right arm, upon hearing the words, "SHAME ON YOU!," and the raising of your right arm. Remember—your tone of voice is important here, so be sure to sound like you're scolding him. After many repetitions, you should be able to eliminate the treats each time (save one until the end of the session), and he should perform this trick with the cues and the command reliably.

Note: With his head "hiding" under your arm, it will appear as if your horse is truly ashamed of himself. This is a great "cover-up" trick, for times when the horse doesn't get a trick right. Your patter and this trick will make people think that he really knows that he's wrong, and he will appear even smarter! This trick can be the ultimate lifesaver— a very useful, face-saving response!

ANSWERING QUESTIONS: Nodding "YES"

Equipment needed: halter, lead rope, carrots, nail and whip, approximately 39" long.

For these next two tricks, nodding "yes," and shaking the head "no," we are going to introduce to the horse the use of a whip, which will be used as a "cue stick," or extension of your hand. If your horse is frightened of a whip, take time and introduce it to him slowly, by showing it to him and letting him smell it (don't ever let him take it in his mouth—it's *your* piece of equipment, not his), gently stroking it on different parts of his body so that he gets used to its feel.

STEP 1: Rehearse the tricks your horse already has learned. Have a halter and lead rope on the horse. Standing about a foot off the horse's left shoulder and facing forward with the lead rope in your left hand, take a pointed object, such as a nail, in your right hand and gently prick him on the chest (*prick, do not jab*—if he bites your hand, you are pricking too hard!). The horse, acting as if a fly bit him on his chest, will bring his head and neck down to bite at the fly. The moment the horse makes any downward movement with his head, reward him with a piece of carrot and praise him lavishly.

Note: Try various places on the chest to get the result you want. Each horse has a spot that is more responsive than another, and you, the trainer, should find the spot that works best for your horse. The nail is the reinforcing aid for this movement. Gradually you will eliminate it. Try twice more, and return your horse to his corral for at least an hour.

STEP 2: Decide what question you want the horse to respond "yes" to. For example, "Do you love me?" Your tone of voice is very important, so make it a *question*. Stand by your horse's left shoulder and cue with the nail on the chest, as before. Your horse should make some movement down and up with his head. For any likeness of a nod, reward him with a carrot and try several more times, rewarding generously. Return him to his corral or stall.

STEP 3: Repeat as in Step 2, only substitute the butt end of the whip for the nail, tapping him with it. Reward often and only return to using the nail if he doesn't respond to the whip. Return him to his stall or corral.

STEP 4: In this final phase, the horse begins to respond to the whip before it actually touches his chest. After he successfully responds several times, reward him and put him away.

Soon, just by pointing the whip at his chest and asking the question, he will respond

Yessiree, Bob!
Photo courtesy of Gary Fletcher

by nodding "yes." After he has mastered this trick with the first question, you can throw any playful question at your horse, and between your body position, the whip cue and your tone of voice, he will answer, "Yessiree, Bob!" Your horse is talking back to you! As you rehearse this trick, and others, you should now begin to diminish the treats, and offer praise only instead. Your horse will come to enjoy the praise as much as the treats, and especially, the knowledge that he is pleasing you!

33

SHAKING THE HEAD "NO"

Equipment needed: halter, lead rope, carrots, nail, whip (same length as before).

This trick is also based on the natural action reflex of a horse shaking his head when a fly bites him on the neck.

STEP 1: Have a halter and lead rope on your horse, standing him in a stall, aisle or alongside a fence. Do not hold his head since this will keep him from shaking it. Stand on the left side of your horse and with the nail in your right hand, prick his neck lightly near the withers, as if a fly is landing on him. Experiment until you find the spot that provokes a head shake. If he shakes his head slightly, reward with pats and praise, and offer him a piece of carrot.

STEP 2: Prick the same spot once more until he responds slightly and reward the same as before. This time add a question requiring a "No" answer, using a certain tone of voice and allowing the last word to fall, for instance, "Are you a bad boy?"

STEP 3: Prick the same spot and as soon as he shakes his head, reward him with a carrot and put him away in his corral or stall for at least an hour. Repeat these steps several times a day, always in the same position by the horse's side or shoulder.

STEP 4: In the correct position, cue the horse with a prick, but use the butt end of the whip to tap him. If he doesn't respond, use the nail to remind him. Praise and reward generously for a correct response. After a short time, your horse should respond to the whip as he sees you move it towards his neck. Spectators will never guess! You should make it absolutely clear to your horse that he is only to do this on command. Do not reward him if he does it "off cue." Now with a stack of questions, your horse will really have "no-how!" With a little imagination, you can involve other people around you, and ask your horse if Aunt Sally is wearing a red dress, and they will be astounded. Think of the conversations the two of you can have!

Note: You will find that some horses do not respond to shaking their heads at the prick on the withers or neck. In these cases, you might try a little higher up, closer to the ears, for the head shake. Some horses, whose nerve endings must be not very close to the skin, are not as responsive as others. With these horses, I would suggest pressing a little harder with a blunt object, and try for the "YES" under the jaw and the "NO" up by the ear. The adept trainer needs to find out what works best for his horse! The "NO" trick will be combined with later tricks in the next chapter. When you have taught the "YES" and "NO" tricks, you will have a head start in teaching the tricks found in Chapter 2.

Who's a bad boy? Not me!
Photo courtesy of Gary Fletcher

PUSHING YOU AROUND

Equipment needed: halter, lead rope, carrots.

Always a pushover!
Photo courtesy of Cynthia McFarland

This trick is one of the easiest tricks there is to teach your horse. He will love it from the first since he feels he is getting the chance to push you around for a change! And this is exactly what you want him to do. An excellent time to teach this trick is just before feeding time, letting him push you into the feed room. The horse may be given one to four lessons a day in learning this trick.

STEP 1: Hold a small piece of carrot in either hand, tease him a little with it and turn your back to him. Hold the hand with the carrot in it behind your back and get him to lower his head even with or lower than your shoulders. Lean against his face, gently. He will probably nudge you slightly as if to say, "Hey, get off of me!" Reward him at the first sign of resistance.

STEP 2: Repeat Step 1, leaning a little heavier against him and make him push you out of his way so he can get a carrot. Tell him, "PUSH!"

STEP 3: As soon as he has pushed you one step, make him push you two the next time. Let him nudge you forward and then stagger backward immediately to lean on him again. Add the command, "PUSH!" when you lean on him. Withhold the reward a little longer each time.

Note: If you are training a stallion or a mouthy gelding, be careful that he does not bite at you or your clothing. Your horse should continue to push as long as your back is toward him and you continue to stagger backward. His cue to stop pushing is when you turn to face him. Then pet him and let him know the "playtime" is over.

You can continue to refine your cues, by saying the word, "PUSH!," and turning your back to him, standing directly in front of him. You can progress to doing without a halter and lead rope once he has mastered this trick with it on.

A caution applies to this trick: Although it is delightful, if you or others are not aware that by standing in front of the horse with your back towards him while leading him, that you are giving him the cue to "PUSH," you will undoubtedly be shoved by your horse, having taught him this trick. You and others handling your horse should be aware of the implications some trick behaviors will have, otherwise they will become nuisance behaviors in no time flat. Some tricks will have warning labels! I used to use this trick to demonstrate how my horse would show me the way home when we got lost on a trail ride in the woods.

Rehearse your horse regularly, above all, demand obedience, as this can mean success or failure. Now you have a horse that can really use his head! 🐎

CHAPTER 2

From the Horse's Mouth

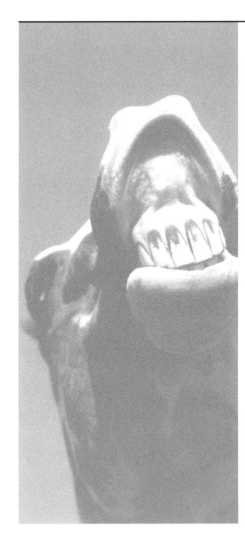

If you have tried the suggested training methods in the previous chapter, you have probably successfully trained your horse to use his head for performing tricks. While we are working with his head, it naturally follows to train the horse to use his mouth to perform some entertaining tricks.

There are so many amusing and clever tricks a horse can do with his mouth alone. The horse's mouth is almost as versatile as the human hand. He can pick up and hold things, carry items, fetch and retrieve, wave objects (like a flag), push or roll objects, such as carriages and barrels, untie knots, twirl a rope, pull off blankets, play basketball, pick up trash, jump rope, drink from a bottle and smile. The possibilities are endless, and it only takes your imagination to conjure up a routine you can do with this series alone. I have taught horses to "pick out" the number cards I ask for, turn light on and off, take a tissue out of a box and hand it to me, and numerous other fun tricks.

I've seen a "drunk act" performed by great comedian/trick horse trainers, that used tricks involving the horse's mouth almost exclusively!

In this series, you should be careful not to damage the horse's mouth with anything too pointy, jagged or heavy. You do not want to cause any damage to the horse's teeth, mouth or gums. Be sure that whatever you ask him to handle with his mouth is clean and dirt-free. Keep a hanky either soaked in apple juice or carrots handy so that it absorbs the odor of the treat and will be enticing to your horse.

Keep your training sessions brief, continue regularity, and be certain your horse has mastered each trick before moving on the the next one. Ideally, you should rehearse the previously-learned tricks at least once a day. Just be sure that you have taught well whatever it is you have taught, otherwise the horse will end up confused.

LIP SERVICE: The Smile

Equipment needed: halter, lead rope, ammonia, nail, feather, carrots.

This trick usually brings roars of laughter from people, and will even bring a smile to your face. Many horses curl up their upper lips when they smell something strange, or when a stallion, for example, smells a mare in heat. It appears when they turn up their upper lip that they are smiling or laughing.

STEP 1: Outfit your horse in a halter and lead rope, standing him in a stall, aisle, or next to a fence. Stand directly in front of him, and place a strange-smelling odor, such as ammonia or a cut onion, under his nostrils, and tell him, "SMILE!" Generally, with most horses, this strong odor will achieve the desired effect. If he does not react to the strong odor, try tickling him on the upper lip with a feather or lightly pricking the upper lip with a nail to get it to curl.

STEP 2: Reward your horse with a piece of carrot when he rolls back his lip, even ever so slightly in the beginning, and generously praise him.

STEP 3: Repeat Steps 1 and 2 over and over again for as many BRIEF sessions as it takes, until your horse is conditioned to roll back his lip whenever your finger approaches his muzzle and you say the word, "SMILE!"

Some horses have very agile lips, and some just turn them up slightly, as if they are "grinning." You and your horse will both enjoy this trick, and now you can show off his "Colgate" smile. Your horse has learned the body cue of standing in front of him and the hand cue in front of his face together with the command, "SMILE!" You can practice this trick often, whenever you go out to the corral or to the barn. It's easy, because you don't need a whip for this trick, just your hand and a carrot. You can even ask others to make your horse smile, since they don't have to touch him and will get a lot of pleasure from seeing him laugh.

You will start to notice that your horse is beginning to learn faster. That is because he is learning how to learn, what you expect of him, and what he can expect from you.

A "Colgate" Smile!
Photo courtesy of Cynthia McFarland

THE PICKPOCKET: Taking a Hanky from Your Pocket!

Equipment needed: halter, lead rope, hanky, carrots.

Photo courtesy of Gary Fletcher

No book on tricks written during this age of political surprises would be complete without a trick such as this one. The winning combination is this: A horse's natural and beautiful innocence added to the low trickery, deceit and sneakiness that are too often a part of human nature as we find it in our times. So if you enjoy dirty tricks, have fun with this one.

This hanky trick, as well as the succeeding ones involv-ing the horse's mouth, will utilize objects that the horse will handle with his teeth. Make certain that they are safe for him to handle, and that he is not afraid of them. They should be large enough so that he cannot eat or swallow them, and free from any dirt. Use articles that you don't care about your horse ruining, because he will tear some of them in these early lessons. When he takes the hanky from your pocket, he may tear the pocket, so wear "barn clothes" you don't mind having torn.

I take my hanky and put it in a container with carrots, so that it absorbs the smell of the carrot thoroughly and will be more interesting to the horse. Every trick using the horse's mouth begins with this first hanky trick, so take your time and teach this trick well to your horse. Don't skip this essential trick, as this hanky will reappear often in more complex tricks using the horse's mouth. If you do not teach this trick now, in this stage of his trick-training, you will need to go back and teach it later.

STEP 1: Place a piece of carrot on a hanky that you are holding in your hand, while the other hand is holding on to the lead rope attached to the halter, stand-ing directly in front of your horse. Show him the carrot and let him eat it and a few more pieces from the hanky. He should begin to identify the hanky with the carrot.

STEP 2: Repeat Step 1, this time, saying to your horse, "TAKE THE HANKY!"

STEP 3: When your horse is reliably taking the hanky from your hand, then take the hanky with a small piece of carrot inside of it, and, with most of it hanging out of your pants pocket, turn and tell him, "TAKE THE HANKY!" emphasizing the word hanky.

When he does, reward him with a piece of carrot. By this time, he should try and remove the hanky, but if he doesn't, return to Steps 1 and 2. For now, keep using the same pocket. Repeat this a number of times until the horse knows that he will only get the carrot when he removes the hanky from your pocket.

STEP 4: Repeat Step 3, only this time keep changing pockets from which he must remove the hanky: front pants pocket, behind pockets, side pockets, shirt and coat pock-ets. He should be confirmed in removing the hanky from whatever pocket you ask him to when you command, "TAKE THE HANKY!" Always stress the word, *hanky*.

Note: Most horses think grabbing the hanky out of your pocket is a lot of fun! They even get real excited, so watch that their teeth don't take a nip out of you! Whenever you place an object on your body and ask the horse to use his teeth to get it, you must exercise caution. He doesn't mean to hurt you with his teeth— he just may get very eager!

I use this "pickpocket" trick in my routine to take a wallet, checkbook, or almost any-thing else I dream of having the horse remove. Be sure your horses understands to do this only on cue, or you'll have a horse that is constant-ly at your pockets, and this will then become a nuisance behavior.

By working to this extent with the humble hanky, you have actually set the pattern you will be using from this point on. Now that your horse will pick up some-thing with his mouth, we will later increase the variety of articles he picks up, such as a hat, flag, shirt, bottle, or ball. We will also start to combine tricks.

HATS OFF TO YOU!
Taking a Hat Off Your Head and Give It to You!

Equipment needed: halter, lead rope, hat, carrots.

Use a hat that you have worn and has your scent on it. Your horse will recognize your scent as that of someone he loves and trusts. A felt hat is soft and absorbs your odor well, won't tear as easily as straw, and isn't as scratchy.

This trick has several elements in it: Your horse will learn to take something in his mouth, hold it in his mouth and then give it to you (without dropping it). Each element should be taught carefully, until the horse does them well.

STEP 1: With a halter and lead rope on your horse, standing just off to the side of him a little and facing him, hold a hat with the crown dished in at the top with a few pieces of carrot in it, and offer it to him, commanding, "TAKE MY HAT!" Let him eat the carrots. Repeat this a number of times, petting him.

STEP 2: Repeat Step 1 a few times until your horse actually takes the hat in his

Hold it!

Photo courtesy of Gary Fletcher

mouth. When he does take it with his teeth, take the hat from him and give him the carrot with the other hand. He is learning that the reward comes as a result of his taking the hat in his mouth (like the hanky).

STEP 3: Offer the horse your hat by the brim. He should take it, and as soon as he takes the hat in his mouth, tell him, "Hold it!," holding your hand under his jaw. Take it from him and reward him. Don't let him drop the hat. Repeat this a few times until he holds the hat for you to take it from him. If he drops the hat, scold him, get the hat and begin again. Never reward him if he drops the hat.

STEP 4: When your horse is reliably taking the hat from your hand, holding it, and you are taking it from him, put the hat on your head and bend down in front of him,

putting the hat close to your horse's mouth. Say, "TAKE MY HAT!." He should take it right off your head, but if he doesn't, put some carrots in the dish of the hat to entice him. You probably won't need to put the feed in the hat since you have already taught him to take it by the brim (watch out for his teeth when he grabs the hat off your head!).

STEP 5: When your horse is confirmed in taking the hat off your head, drop it on the ground right in front of him and say,"Pick up my hat!" If he doesn't pick it up right away, pick it up yourself and hold the hat a foot off the ground and let him take it from that place several times. Then drop it back on the ground, and pointing to it, command him to pick it up. Repeat until he picks the hat up from the ground and say, "GIVE IT TO ME," reaching for it and making him give it

to you before giving him a treat. Repeat this until he does it well (this may take many repetitions).

STEP 6: Toss the hat a few feet away and tell him, "Go get my hat!," pointing to the hat and pushing him towards it. Now, your horse may not initially do this at first, because he has not previously learned to walk away from you. Now he must learn to go in the direction you point, and the command, "Go!" (this is a retrieving skill).

STEP 7: Take your horse by the lead rope and walk him over to the hat. When you ask him to pick it up he should do so immediately because he already knows how to do this. When he picks it up with his mouth, walk away from him and go

back to the place where you first commanded him to "go" and make him bring it to you. Don't give him the treat if he drops it before you reach for it. He'll probably follow you back with the hat in between his teeth. If he drops the hat or refuses to pick it up, start over again tossing the hat from the same place. If he does bring it back to you, pet him, praise him lavishly and give him a carrot.

STEP 8: Once he has mastered picking up the hat from a few feet away, toss it anywhere, and have him pick it up and return it to you, rewarding him generously for his efforts. Now, you have a horse that will carry and retrieve—your very own "golden retriever!" The hat is a good article to

begin retrieving since it is light and easy to carry. There are many things that he can learn to retrieve.

Note: Now try having your horse take the hat off someone else's head and give it to you. You can also teach him to take it back to the owner with a little work. You may need to show him a few times, but he will do it. When he does return the hat to the person, tell them to give him a carrot. This trick is useful in that you are teaching your horse to go away from you and return. People will be amazed at his intelligence!

I like to have my horse "tip his hat" to a lady and "kiss" her— shows how polite he is. Maybe you can get Merlin to even pull a rabbit out of your hat!

THE PATRIOTIC HORSE: Waving a Flag!

Equipment needed: halter, lead rope, hanky, small 11"x16" stick flag, whip, carrots.

This trick is a combination trick, using the HEAD NODDING "YES" from Chapter 1, with the hanky, as in the PICK-POCKET trick. The horse will hold the flag in his mouth, and make a "waving" movement with it, by giving him the cue for nodding his head "YES."

STEP 1: Rehearse your horse in giving the head nod, "YES." Also refresh his memory in taking the hanky from your hand. When he does both of these tricks consistently, outfit your horse in a halter and lead rope, and standing at his left shoulder, hold the lead rope in your left hand. Command your horse, "TAKE THE HANKY!" Make him hold it in his mouth by holding your hand under his jaw. If he drops it, hold it in his mouth so that he can't

drop it, pet him and tell him, "Hold it!"

STEP 2: As soon as your horse has the hanky in his mouth, ask him a "YES" question, giving him the "YES" cue. When he holds the hanky in his mouth and nods, pet him and give him a carrot.

STEP 3: Repeat Step 2 a few times. Offer your horse the hanky, and command, "WAVE THE HANKY!," giving him the "YES" cue. As soon as he has waved it just once, take it back and give him a carrot. Teach him to continue to wave it until you take the hanky from him. With the whip giving him the cue to nod, he should move the hanky around quite a bit. Try experimenting with the "NO" cue as well, and see which waving motion you prefer with the hanky.

Don't expect him to wave it too long— a few seconds will do just fine.

STEP 4: Wrap the hanky around the flag handle. Practice having the horse hold the flag with the hanky wrapped around it in his mouth and tell him, "TAKE THE FLAG!" When he is comfortably holding the flag wrapped with the hanky in his mouth, give him the cue to nod his head for the waving motion. He should wave the flag pretty well, since he has the hanky to "grip" on to. When he is doing it well with the hanky, remove the hanky and try it without the hanky, commanding him to "WAVE THE FLAG!" Reward him generously for his efforts. Practice this trick several times a day, without overdoing it, and your horse will be a flag-waver in no time!

Flag-waving horse!
Photo courtesy of Cynthia McFarland

Note: You can *really* capitalize on a horse's natural talents with this trick, especially if he likes to be playful with his mouth. My stallion devilishly waves the hanky around as if to say, "Ah-ha!—I've got your hanky and now it's mine!" Same with a flag. Now you're ready to take your horse to a ball game and sing the National Anthem!

Make sure each component of this trick is mastered before combining them as a unit.

Think up a situation for using these tricks and chances are you will come up with your own humorous lines for them. Work on your delivery of these lines— your horse's performance depends on how well you present him!

BOTTOMS UP! Drinking from a Bottle

Equipment needed: halter, lead rope, whip, plastic unbreakable bottle, carrots.

Want a drink!
Photo courtesy of Cynthia McFarland

Up until this point, all that you have taught the horse to pick up with his mouth has been pretty easy for him to learn and just as easy for you to teach. The articles continue to be light to carry in his mouth. He has learned to hold them in his mouth and not to drop them. In this lesson, he will learn to take a bottle in his mouth and hold it up in the air, as if he is drinking from it. Use a light-weight PLASTIC, unbreakable bottle. Remember to practice with the horse on all that he has learned so far, continuing to offer him carrots for performing correctly.

STEP 1: Outfit your horse in a halter and lead rope, holding the lead rope in your left hand. Standing in front of your horse but over to the side a little, take an empty large plastic bottle (like Coke or Pepsi) with a long mouth, with a carrot sticking out of

it (remove the cap). Place your left hand under your horse's chin, raise his head a bit, and gently insert the bottle in the corner of his mouth. Keep holding his head up as he tries eating the carrot out of the mouth of the bottle. You may have to hold up the bottle. Be careful that he doesn't bite down on the bottle with his teeth. As you offer him the bottle, say, "WANT A DRINK?", emphasizing the word *drink*.

STEP 2: Repeat Step 1 several times, using the same bottle every time, and making sure it has a carrot in it.

STEP 3: When your horse takes the bottle in his mouth and holds it up in drinking position, instead of holding your hand under his chin, point the whip under his chin as a cue to hold up his head, and ask, "WANT A DRINK?"

STEP 4: Repeat Step 3, eliminating the carrot from the mouth of the bottle. Reward your horse for taking the bottle and holding his head up. Repeat this several times until he has mastered it well.

Note: Your horse will come to recognize this bottle as "his." I am amazed at how my horse looks at a strange bottle, knowing it is not the one we generally use. You can use this trick to ask him if he wants a drink on a hot day, or if he'd like to go to a party and have a drink. Or you can use it as part of a "drunk" act. It is up to you to think up some witty remarks to fit in around this trick. After all, your horse is making YOU look good, why shouldn't you take the time to think what will make HIM look great! This trick is not so difficult as it is repetitious to teach. You can combine this trick with the "push" trick, and use it as the drunkard's shove. Depending upon your patter, it makes for an entertaining act.

FINAL THOUGHTS

Photo courtesy of Cynthia McFarland

You have now completed with your horse the ABCs of trick-training. You can have a complete dialogue with your horse, and put on a little "show" with him. More importantly, you have established the basis for his further education. He is learning how to learn, that is, to reason and to think. He is learning how to respond to cues, commands, body position and tone of voice. He is giving you his undivided attention and knows that by listening he will get a reward. Amazing what the reward system of training has produced in your horse so far—a wonder horse!

The two of you are really learning how to communicate with each other. You are developing a bond between the two of you of love, trust, respect and obedience. You are beginning to learn each other's dispositions and limitations. You are both ready to continue on and further his education using other parts of his body, now that you have completed this level of training. Congratulations, graduate! You are acquiring quite a repertoire!

Photo courtesy of Cynthia McFarland

CHAPTER 3

What a Feat!

In the last two chapters, for tricks involving the horse's head, neck and mouth, you used the whip as a "cue stick" for many movements. In this next section of lessons involving the horse's feet and legs, you will be using the whip for every trick, as if it were an extension of your hand. In this way, you will not need to bend over to point, and it will be a much more subtle cue, not amateurish, but just like the professionals.

This is an appropriate time to mention the use of discipline, which may involve the use of your whip. There will be times when you will need to use it as mild discipline or to tap your horse sharply to make him understand what you want him to do. It would be naive to think that as much as you love your horse, that he won't disobey or not pay attention. He will, and at that very time, he will need to feel the whip. I am not referring to a whipping, but rather to a sharp reprimand with a strong tap of the whip. After he has stopped to your satisfaction, you can soften your voice and remind him you still love him. Since he already has reasoning powers, he will figure out what the discipline was for if meted out IMMEDIATELY. He knows that the discipline is tempered with love. The whip is part of your equipment used for giving the horse signals, and not something he should touch or play with. Keep his mouth off of it. It's yours, not his. Now on to some challenging fun with your horse!

HOW DO YOU DO?
Shaking Hands

Equipment needed: halter, lead rope, soft cotton lead rope with snap, whip, carrots.

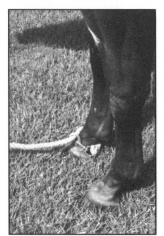

It is customary for people to shake hands when greeting. When you greet a horse, the only difference is that you shake a hoof instead. With dogs, shaking a paw is an oldie but goodie, a real classic. But while it is old hat to some folks with dogs, it's real impressive when you see a big horse offer his foot. You will get a lot of mileage out of this trick. Trust me.

Photos courtesy of Gary Fletcher

A horse will lift his hoof on a number of occasions without knowing this trick. He will paw if he is impatient, anxious or wants attention. So let's put this behavior on cue and put it to work for you, so you can show off how Harpo greets people.

For this trick and for some of the others in this series, you will use a long, soft cotton lead rope with a big snap around the horse's ankle. If your horse is not accustomed to having anything on his legs (like shipping boots, bell boots, even easy boots or horseshoes), or having his feet handled, then take some time getting him used to a soft lead rope around his ankle. Practice pulling up his hoof, until he is relaxed and unafraid.

STEP 1: With a halter and lead rope on your horse, and standing your horse next to a fence or wall by his right side, stand directly in front of him, facing him, with the long, soft cotton lead rope tied around his right ankle by the snap. Make sure the snap or rope is padded enough not to hurt him. Holding the lead rope in your right hand, say, "SHAKE," gently pulling your horse's right leg up. Catch his right foot with your right hand and "shake hands." Reward him with a piece of carrot. Repeat several times, giving him a carrot every time his foot is pulled up.

STEP 2: Repeat Step 1 a few times, making sure that you say your commands like *commands*. As you pull his foot up with the rope, tap him on the outside of the right ankle, and hold his foot up, resting it on your knee, stroking his leg and feeding him his carrot with your left hand. Make him understand that extending your right hand towards his right leg is the cue (same is true for people!).

STEP 3: Repeat Step 2, dispensing with the rope, and just pointing the whip, tapping his right ankle, saying, "SHAKE." Reward him when he raises his foot. If he hesitates to lift his foot, tap his right leg sharply on the cannon bone. Be patient, but firm. After all, this is the first step in teaching him how to use his legs and feet. It may also be his first experience with the whip causing a sting! Even though mild, it sets the tone for the rest of the tricks involving the feet, legs and the bite of the whip.

STEP 4: Repeat Step 3, extending your right hand to his right leg, and continue rewarding, until the offering of your right hand and command, "SHAKE," produces an immediate "handshake."

Note: Teach this trick well, and rehearse all of the others before proceeding on to the next one. You can also use this trick to ask your horse to "GIVE YOU FIVE," which as I'm sure you know is when you offer your open palm and someone else slaps it. With the command, "GIVE ME FIVE," offer your open palm and your horse will offer the shaking hands movement, which is close enough to make it look good. It gives the shaking hands a new twist, with a modern look.

You can also teach this trick with the left leg as well. Then you could tell your horse to shake with his left foot, and show how he knows right from left. This will let you jazz up a neat trick which your patter can make very effective.

THAT FIGURES! Counting

Equipment needed: halter, lead rope, whip, carrots.

If your horse counts, you can do some of the most mind-boggling, amusing and fun tricks with him. You can use audience participation to offer Einstein math problems that he will count out the answer to. Just remember, *you* have to be able to work without a calculator!

STEP 1: With a halter and lead rope on your horse, stand him next to a fence or wall. Stand at his left shoulder, facing in the same direction as him, lead rope in your left hand and the whip in your right hand. Tap the horse's left front ankle with the whip, as though it were a fly, and tell him, "COUNT." He will stomp his left foot to try and get rid of the pesky fly. Give him a carrot when he lifts his foot and puts it back down.

STEP 2: Repeat Step 1 several times. Increase the number of times you ask the horse to count, gradually rewarding him after he has pawed or stomped a few times.

STEP 3: Repeat Step 2 several times. This time, ask your horse a question, such as, "How old are you?" If he is six years old, tap him so that he will stomp his foot six times, then reward him. Be sure he stomps no more than his age. When you want him to stop counting, take a step forward, and he will immediately stop. The step forward will be the cue to stop counting. You can practice this trick by asking your horse to add, subtract, multiply or divide. Keep his attention on your right hand and the motion of the little whip. If he becomes too confused by too many different problems, return to using just one until he has learned it well. Remember to reward him for the right answers.

And, it's one, two, three!
Photo courtesy of Gary Fletcher

You will refine your cue to standing at his left shoulder and merely pointing the whip at his left ankle and using a command or question, your tone of voice which he will come to understand. To stop counting, your cue will be a step forward, which people will hardly notice. He won't even be looking at you and will count on cue.

Note: If your horse does not respond to the cue on his ankle, you can also cue him by tapping the butt end of the whip on his chest, above his foreleg. Sometimes, they will respond to that place as well.

You can present this trick in a multitude of ways: you can ask your horse to count others' ages (be careful he doesn't tell yours!), buttons on clothes, even do magic tricks with numbers. The possibilities are endless! It's all in how you present a trick which can either make it or break it. This leads me to the following discussion on "Showmanship."

SHOWMANSHIP

At this point it's only fair to tell you that it will be YOUR job to make your horse look good, since he is making you look good. What if he does goof? What if he gives the wrong answer? He can't ad-lib his way out of the situation, but you can. Your gift of gab can make this counting trick, or others, look great. Be prepared to correct him in a way your audience won't spot as a correction. Cover up for him—he's your pal. If you ask him how many months there are in a year, and he counts out 14, ask him if he's on the same calendar you are. If he counts out your incorrect age, say, "You forgot my last two birthdays, you doll." Only your patter can punch this trick up to the limelight it deserves, or any others, for that matter. Or, if you are doing a demonstration, you can end up with a funny number question such as, "How old am I?" and stop the horse before he counts out the tragic truth by saying, "I'm afraid we're out of time now." You are only limited by your own imagination and wit.

CALISTHENICS FOR HORSES: Stretching

Equipment needed: halter or bridle, lead rope, whip, carrots.

Doesn't he look majestic and proud?
Photo courtesy of Gary Fletcher

This is an important trick for a well-rounded repertoire. Since you will, in his advanced trick-training education, teach him to lie down (go to bed at night), this trick will demonstrate what he does when he gets up in the morning (stretches). With the first two tricks in this series, shaking hands and counting, only one foot and leg were involved. This trick, stretching, involves the use of all four feet and is the precurser to tricks using the horse's entire body. It's great for conditioning, too.

It is a lovely pose that teaches your horse to stand still and hold a pose, much like the park of an Arabian, Morgan or Saddlebred. The horse's head and neck, front legs, barrel and hind legs are all positioned in place. It is a great position to mount or dismount from, making the stirrup hang lower and easier for getting up on his back (unless you have a mini or pony). In the beginning, I would not recommend holding the pose for any longer than a couple of minutes, for the horse's back may not be too strong. He needs to build up his back muscles for mounting and dismounting. Just be careful not to overdo at first, or you will weaken the horse.

STEP 1: Have a halter and lead rope or bridle on your horse, and stand him next to a wall or fence on his right side. You should stand at his left shoulder, facing the shoulder with the lead rope or reins in your left hand, holding it under the horse's chin. Position his head up higher than his back, with his chin raised, and holding him in this position, reward him and say, "Head up!" Keep reminding him to "hold it," since it is critical that he hold his head in position. If he tries to drop it, tap him under the chin with the whip to remind him. When you put it back in place,

reward him for "holding." With practice, you won't need to tap quite so sharply, and he'll understand what the whip under his chin means (he already has had the whip under his chin for holding the bottle and flag up in the previous chapter).

STEP 2: Repeat Step 1 over and over, until your horse has learned to position his head and hold it. Then tap his left front foot behind the ankle with the whip in your right hand, and at the same time, touch his pastern on that foot with your boot toe, so that he moves it forward a step, and tell him to "STRETCH." Reward him when he does take a step forward, and make him hold this position, petting and praising him the whole time he is in this position. Repeat getting his left foot in position a number of times and reward him. Put him away in a stall or corral.

STEP 3: Rehearse the left foot taking a step forward. Reach under his belly with the whip and tap his right leg in the same place as you did with the left (he should transfer the cues from one leg to the other). Move his right foot forward by pressing your boot toe on it same as you did with the left foot, and moving it up even with the left, telling him to "STRETCH." Have him hold this position while you reward him with a carrot and praise. Repeat this procedure a number of times until he is moving his right foot in place well.

STEP 4: Repeat Steps 2 and 3 until your horse is stretching his front feet out well before proceeding to back him out of the stance. Don't let him step forward with his hind feet, even though this will ease the back muscles. Always back him out of the stretch so he doesn't creep up with his hind feet.

STEP 5: When your horse is holding his head up and taking a couple of steps forward with both feet, practice this a few times, asking now for four or five steps (no more than five) in a stretching pose and to hold that pose for a couple of minutes. Always walk him forward a bit, turn him around, and get him in a stand where his hind feet are even and try the pose a couple of more times. Don't overdo it—he is building up those back muscles. Reward him when he has achieved the beautiful stance you are after. Doesn't he look majestic and proud!

Note: After your horse is thoroughly confirmed in this trick, you might try mounting him from the ground in this stretch. I usually mount from the stretch or the bow positions.

Before proceeding on to the next trick, rehearse your horse with all that you have taught him up to this point. Your horse by now is accustomed to getting rewarded for his tricks, responding to your tone of voice commands, body position and cues with the whip. He trusts you so that even when he feels the "bite" of the whip or the pull of the rope on his ankle, he knows you will not hurt him. You have established a wonderful foundation for moving on to more complicated movements. You will be able to rely on him to perform for you out of desire and trust.

A WORD ABOUT TREATS...

Don't be a food junkie!
Photo courtesy of Gary Fletcher

Your big darling has come to expect food treats from you for performing to your wishes. You should start to alternate sessions with food treats and without, so that he doesn't become a "food junkie." Horses are simple creatures and in the presence of food a good part of their concentration is on the food and not on the education.

Using treats to begin a horse on a new trick is fine practice, but if you want real learning to take place, get rid of the treat each time as soon as it is feasible. A horse who works for praise will eventually be working, too, for the love of the work. A horse who works only for food will stay at that level and not advance.

CHAPTER 4

Legs Over Easy!

ACTING DRUNK: Crossing Legs

Equipment needed: halter, lead rope, ankle rope, whip, bell and/or splint boots, carrots.

The beauty of this trick is that with your own creativity you can make the horse look as if he is intoxicated, has to go to the bathroom, or is making the letter "X." It's always good for a laugh, and it is the forerunner to what you can teach your horse later on as a pivot, both on and off of the pedestal. You will also get your horse used to the ankle rope, as you did for the shaking hands trick. It is certainly easier to use the rope than to bend over all of the time, which is hard on your back. Besides, it is good for your horse to get accustomed to having his ankles, hooves and legs handled. Just don't get caught up in the rope. The stall is the ideal place to teach this trick because if the horse moves around, he can't go off too far.

STEP 1: Outfit your horse in a halter and lead rope, bell and/or splint boots. Stand his right side next to a wall, fence, or in an aisle. Put the soft, long cotton lead rope with the snap around his right ankle, holding it up with your hand. Stand at his left shoulder, facing forward, and pull gently so that his right foot crosses over the left, commanding him to "CROSS." The protective bell and/or splint boots prevent your horse from getting scratches or injuries to his feet or legs. When the right foot is crossed over the left, and rests across the cannon bone, pet and reward him with a carrot. Repeat this procedure several times.

STEP 2: Repeat Step 1 several times. There should be less pulling on the rope the more your horse understands he is supposed to

pick up the right foot and cross it over. You can also try picking up the right foot with your hand and placing it over the left one. Now add the tap of the whip on the right ankle to the pull of the rope, as you say "CROSS." Pet and reward the horse when his right foot crosses the left. Keep repeating until he moves his foot by himself when you tap and command.

STEP 3: Repeat Step 2. Remove the ankle rope and merely use the whip and the command as the cues to have your horse cross the right foot over the left. Have him hold the pose, so he doesn't rush to return to standing on all four feet. This will prepare him for adding some more movement later on to this trick. It will also help him to balance himself on three feet.

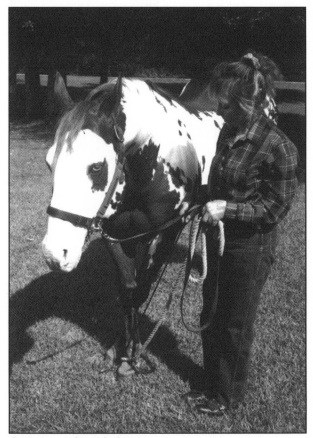

Photo courtesy of Gary Fletcher

Note: As you will see, some tricks will be combined to others, so that you end up building two tricks into very impressive (and usually athletic) poses. Your horse will improve his gymnastic prowess as you increase his muscle strength and powers of reasoning. In this way, your training is like building blocks of learning.

BOW-LEGGED: Taking a Bow on One Knee

Equipment needed: bridle, western saddle or surcingle, saddle pad, whip, bell and/or splint boots, carrots.

Take a message...I'm tied up at the moment.

Photo courtesy of Gary Fletcher

The bow is another of the traditional tricks that all trick horses are supposed to know. It will be the finale of your demonstration, an acknowledgement of your audience's applause. It is also your last chance to win the audience over! Performed well, it's a good trick, but not a heart stopper. Since animal trainers want to end with one of their flashier tricks, pick your most impressive trick and announce that it will be your last. After you perform it and while the crowd is still in a roar, slip in the bow. The trick will be successful because you didn't use it as a feat of amazement, but as a touch of good manners.

If you think about it, your horse already "bows" instinctively when he wants some grass under the fence, for example, or when he starts to lie down. Now, to get him to learn it on cue.

The bow is usually done with the horse's left knee, because we generally mount from the left side, and as you will see later on, it makes the next few tricks easier for both you and your horse. In teaching one trick, I know to plan ahead for future tricks, by training particular legs and cues in a proper order. By teaching the bow on the left knee, you will be well prepared to teach the kneel on both knees, lying down and sitting up.

I like to teach this trick in a clean box stall large enough for the horse to lie down, but confined enough so that he can't move away much. There should be a good amount of soft bedding, so he won't hurt his knee or leg (don't use grass, as this will only distract him). You will need splint boots for his front legs to protect them. A surcingle can be used instead of the western saddle.

STEP 1: Have your horse outfitted in a pad under a western saddle (if using surcingle, without the pad) and a bridle with split reins. Standing in a stall, place the soft, long cotton lead rope

53

around the horse's left front ankle (as you did for previous tricks). Hold the reins of the bridle in your left hand. Stand the horse next to the stall wall, with you standing on his left side, by his shoulder. NEVER stand in front of him or you could get struck

with his legs. With your right hand, pull his left foot up with the rope and let him stand for a minute. Pet him and reward him with a carrot to reasure him the rope won't harm him and he won't have any fear of having his foot held up. This

should take several tries, spaced out in intervals. DON'T hurry this step.

STEP 2: Place the ankle rope through the stirrup, or, if using the surcingle, through the ring. Begin a gentle pull on this left ankle

with the rope through the stirrup and over the horn. Go slow and tell him, "BOW." Let him smell the carrot from your left hand and use it to coax his head down towards his chest as you pull on the rope. The carrot will get his attention

off his body and the horse will often follow it back far enough to actually bow. He may not get his left leg completely down on the ground all the way, and that is just fine. Reward him for any likeness of the bow.

STEP 3: As soon as he bows the first time, remove the ankle rope, pet him and let him rest a few minutes before making him bow again. Twice will be enough the first day—you don't want to strain his muscles. Step 4. Rehearse Steps 2 and 3 in your next session. After he has learned to bow using the gear (the time needed to learn varies with each horse), remove the ankle rope and tap his left knee gently with the whip, command him, "BOW," and the bets are on him bowing the first time. Reward him with a carrot only when his knee is on the ground.

Repeat several times in 15 minute sessions, no longer, and the command,

Photo courtesy of Gary Fletcher

"BOW," the touch of the whip on his left knee and your body position will be his cues to bow on one knee. Just remember to be careful where you do this, and not to overdo, for this and other strenuous tricks can put a strain on the horse's muscles. You will look very professional with this polished cue. You'll see many "amateurs" bending down to have their horses bow on one knee with what I call a "carrot bow." Your cues will be far more subtle and appealing. Prepare for the applause to be a standing ovation. You can take a bow too, if you like. It is hard earned and greatly deserved!

Note: When the horse is bowing well in his stall, I then take him out to a soft, sandy dirt paddock or arena and practice bowing there. I teach the horse to stay for longer periods of time in the bow, holding my whip at his knee. The horse should be taught to get up *only* when you tell him to. However, keep the time spent on his knees to a minimum.

To mount your horse from the bow position, while he is down on his left knee, put your left foot in

Encore, encore!
Photo courtesy of Chris Sartre

the stirrup, and with the whip in your left hand and the reins in your right hand and on the pommel of the saddle, stand in the left stirrup, straighten your arms and tell the horse to get up. When the horse is standing on his four feet, you bring your right leg well over the rear of the saddle and ease down into it as you place your right foot in the stirrup. Don't try dismounting from a bow—it's too awkward.

To bow from the saddle, first work with someone on the ground who will stand on the left side of the horse at his shoulder and cue him for a bow as you have taught him. You must lean back a bit, so as to keep your balance while the horse is going down on his knee. It will take some practice, but you will get accustomed to it. When you feel at ease with your ground person giving the cue, then you should try giving your horse the bow cue from the saddle by tapping him on his left knee with the whip. You may need to lean over ever so slightly. With a little bit of practice, you can polish the bow to look very graceful, to be sure!

Keep 'em beggin' for more!
Photo courtesy of Chris Sartre

SAYING PRAYERS:
Kneeling on Two Knees

Equipment needed: bridle, saddle pad, saddle (or surcingle), ankle rope, whip, bell and/or splint boots, carrots.

You are understandably delighted that Star is able to now take a bow. But wait, it gets even better! An outgrowth of teaching the bow on one knee, there is an even better trick that has some snazzy twists: the kneel on both knees. I find with most horses, that after teaching the horse to bow on one knee, if you teach the kneel next, it will come easily, especially if the horse is relaxed. As in the bow, put splint boots on your horse and put him in a large stall with soft bedding so he won't hurt his knees or legs. Outfit your horse in the same gear as for the bow.

STEP 1: Stand by your horse's left shoulder, and with the reins in your left hand, tap the horse with the whip on his left knee, telling him to "BOW." Just as his left leg is on the ground (your timing needs to be good), reach across his chest and tap his right knee, telling him to "PRAY!" Most horses will just draw the right leg back into the kneel position (transferring what was done on the left knee). Try this method a few times. If the horse does kneel with his right leg down, let him get up and quickly reward him with a carrot and praise him generously. Walk the horse around and repeat again, rewarding right away. Only try this three times during the first session, so that you don't overdo it and tire him out.

If your horse does not bring his right leg back when you tap it at first, and tries to bring his head up, tap him under the chin and tell him no, to PRAY, and keep tapping his right knee, being firm with him and not letting him get up. He should respond to this because now he is using his reasoning powers that tell him that a tap on the left knee means to bring that leg under him, so a tap on the right knee must mean to do the same thing with his right leg.

STEP 2: Once the horse is kneeling on both knees, you can move his head into a position for the prayer, by putting a carrot in your hand, encouraging him to reach for it at his chest, and feeding it to him there. This will take some patience and practice to get this right. Tell him to "PRAY," and hold him there for longer and longer periods of time, keeping the whip on his knees. This is also called the ARABIAN PRAYER. When you are ready for him to get up, tell him, "AMEN." This will be his cue to rise.

As with the bow, limit your practice sessions to fifteen minutes so you don't strain your horse's muscles having him kneel on both knees.

Now you can play with this trick. Your prayer (or his, if you prefer), will be limited only by your sense of humor. He can pray for dinner, for a pretty girl horse, for a raise in salary for his master. Gradually build his patience so that you can fool around with longer and longer prayers. It will be a very impressive skill if one day you and your horse have an audience with the Pope.

If your horse does not respond after several days of teaching him to kneel from these steps, you will need to follow the steps in teaching the bow, reversing the sides. Once you have the kneel down from the right side, you can ask on the left side of the horse for the bow on one knee and on the right side for the kneel. Once the horse thoroughly understands both of these tricks, you can ask for either one with you on either side.

To kneel from the saddle while mounted, the cue for the kneel is to tap the horse on the right knee, giving him slack with the reins so that he can go down, and then reach down with the whip, tapping the left knee as well. You will need to sit back so you are not thrust forward. It feels awkward at first, but with practice, you will get used to this position, as with the bow. As the horse does this movement many times, he will become more confident knowing where to put the weight on his knees, especially with a rider in the saddle. Be sure the ground you are using outside or in an arena is soft for his knees, but without any grass.

Variations: THE CAMEL STRETCH

If you want your horse to do a CAMEL STRETCH, instead of pulling his head to his chest, pull his head forward with his chin to the ground, holding and feeding him the carrot there. Make your horse extend his head out by holding the whip under his chin, telling him to "CAMEL STRETCH." The horse should relax and bring his body closer to the ground, bringing his elbow to rest on the back part of the front heels. Be quick to reward the horse for this graceful pose.

Note: In training the horse to do tricks, as in most training, sometimes the horse will show a tendency to do something on his own. My Paint stallion, upon learning to kneel, put one side of his cheek to the ground. He appeared as if he were "begging." I encouraged this placement of his head because I thought I could use it in my act. Your horse may also exhibit tendencies to do a trick in his own style. You can either encourage or discourage it.

PLAYING DEAD: Lying Down

Equipment needed: bridle, whip, bell and/or splint boots, carrots.

Once your horse has mastered the kneel, lying down is quite easy to teach. For this trick, your horse should remain motionless as he lies on his side with his head down. He is steadier and less likely to move lying on his side than lying on his stomach. And besides, it has a better effect. It's hard to pretend he's playing "dead" when he is lying on his stomach. This trick can go into orbit with the right twist. Be sure your training area or *large* stall is covered with soft, deep bedding, as you did for the kneel. This trick can be enjoyable for the horse since he likes rolling periodically, but it also puts him in a vulnerable position from which he cannot easily escape. Make sure he is away from other distractions such as other horses, animals, loud noises or strange objects. You will need to have the horse away from the wall or fence. Be careful about your own safety, that he does not fall on you.

STEP 1: Cue your horse for the kneel, telling him "WHOA," and holding the whip on his knees. Standing at his left shoulder, take the right rein and bring his head well over to the right, having him hold it there for a few seconds. Reward him, and let him get up. Don't try to get him to lie down in the same session or in the same day.

Repeat this several times, until he is relaxed and holding his head to the right in the kneel position. Always reward him, letting him get up afterwards.

STEP 2: Repeat Step 1. When the horse is relaxed with his head to the right in the kneel position, steadily and gently pull his head around even more to the right, tapping him lightly with the whip on the left shoulder, telling him, "LIE DOWN." He will probably relax slowly, losing his balance and just go over on his left side. If he stiffens up and tries to get up, you should go back to the kneel position. In a short while after giving the cues above, he will start to go to a lying down position by himself. Do not keep repeating this too much, or his knees could get sore and if he is hurt in any way, he will be reluctant to bow, kneel or lie down.

STEP 3: When the horse is lying down, you should keep him there until he is relaxed. You can keep the horse down by just taking the right rein and keeping his head up to the right. Talk to him softly, and pet him in this position, reassuring him all the while he is lying down. You can reward him with a carrot in this position, as long as he is lying quietly on his side.

If he tries to roll, as horses sometimes do, say "WHOA," and take the right rein so his head comes to the right and he cannot move. A few sessions like this and your horse will stay quietly lying on his side for longer periods of time. In time, you can sit or stand on him, or walk around him. Do not repeat this trick so often that you make the horse sore or unhappy to do it. To cue him to get up, I usually cluck to him, and he will get to his feet. I do take caution to get out of his way so he can rise.

Note: You can jazz up this trick, by creating a whole act around it. I have seen a "Dead Horse" routine that had people howling! If you give it time, you will be able to lift his tail or a leg and let it fall to the ground like dead weight. No need to explain the meaning of death to your big actor. Caress him, soothe him with your voice, gradually lift his foreleg and let it drop. Put your fingers over his eyes and make him blink so that he closes them. All the while, tell him "whoa." Think of the fun you'll have bringing him back to life!

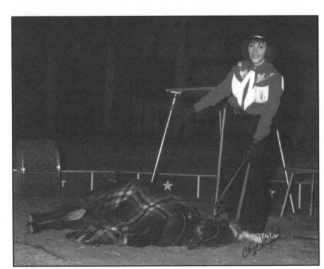
Photo courtesy of Chris Sartre

SIT HAPPENS: Sitting Up

Equipment: bridle, whip, bell and/or splint boots, carrots.

Photo courtesy of Chris Sartre

Don't you wish this trick were as easy to teach to a horse as it is to a dog! Unfortunately, it is a bit more difficult, and may take time and tax your patience. But it is so flashy that it's worth the work!

Training the horse to sit up is usually done after the horse has learned to lie down. Normally, the horse gets up by throwing his front feet out in front. Then he lifts his head and shoulders and brings the front feet back under the front end. He braces his weight on the front legs that are straight out in front of him, and both hind legs are bent as he pushes against them to bring his hind feet more under his body. While doing this his shoulders and part of his barrel are off the ground and his rump is resting on the ground. This is the sit up position.

Your horse should be trained to lie down so well to the point where he enjoys it, and furthermore, trained to where he doesn't jump up hurriedly when you tell him to get up, but is in fact in no hurry to get up. He should be getting to his feet in a leisurely manner and with so much confidence that there is no need to rush it.

STEP 1: Have your horse lie down, as in the previous lesson, in an area that is well-covered with soft sand or bedding, away from a wall or fence. Cluck to the horse to ask the horse to get up. As the horse starts to get up, he will go to this sit up position. Prevent him from rising completely by standing at his left side, telling him to "WHOA," pulling on the reins softly to stop him from getting up any farther. Tell him, "SIT." At first, your horse will probably get up immediately. But after he has done this a few times, he will relax more and listen for your cue to stop. When you horse stops, even momentarily, give him a carrot and praise him generously. Return him to his stall or corral for at least an hour.

STEP 2: Repeat Step 1, asking the horse to stay in the sit position for a bit longer. Reward him with a carrot in this position, but don't overdo it by making him stay there too long.

STEP 3: Repeat Steps 1 and 2, asking the horse to stay in the sit up position for a prolonged period of time. Reward your horse for his efforts.

Note: To make this trick look really spectacular, while the horse is in this sit up position, you can sit between his front legs to show the audience how well-trained he is. Or, when you have taught the horse to sit up with a saddle on, you can stand on the cantle and wave in a grand gesture. In a short while, you can ask your horse to lie down from a mounted position. To do this, cue the horse to bow, then to kneel, then ask the horse to lie down with a ground person giving the same signal you gave from the ground. If you are going to dismount from the horse as the horse lies down, you must take your left foot out of the stirrup, and put it out to the side, stepping out of the way of the horse's body as he lies down. To mount your horse from the sitting position, put your left foot in the stirrup and put the right leg over the saddle and sit in it. You can hold the horn of the saddle (or mane if you ride English), and cluck to your horse to get up. Don't try this on slippery or rocky ground, and be sure not to let the horse eat grass!

At any rate, it's quite impressive, and will bring rave reviews from your audience. If you've gotten this far (without skipping around), you're one heck of a horse trainer! I applaud you! 🎵

Phew! Wow, now on to the next level!
Photo courtesy of Michelle Younghans

CHAPTER 5

Under the Big Top— Circus Tricks

What makes those circus horses so energetic and appealing? What keeps them going two shows a day, seven days a week? Part of the secret is applause. Like people, horses work for applause. Many horses love nothing better than to ham it up before an audience, the larger the better. Some horses will make pleasant or amusing additions to their routines in response to audience feedback. Perhaps you've even noticed your own horse repeating a goof that once got him a laugh. If your horse is capable of cracking jokes, by all means teach him some circus tricks and let him ad-lib.

Circus horses, not unlike yours and mine, need to be seasoned troupers. Your horse will need gradual exposure to crowds before he thrives on being a crowd pleaser. As you build his repertoire of tricks, take him out to noisy places as much as you can to prepare him for life under the spotlights. Even if your own big clown never decides to run away with the circus, it will help season him for performing in front of Aunt Ethel and Uncle Joe or at a special dinner for the Miami Dolphins. Whatever audience you choose, if you play your cards right, your horse will not only perform like a trouper, but he'll enjoy every minute of it and ask to come back. So have a good time—as he will—and don't forget to clap and cheer.

CURTSY BOW

Equipment needed: bridle, whip, saddle/saddle pad (optional), carrots.

This trick is a standby for any circus act, and will add a dramatic touch to your demonstration. It can be done both dismounted or mounted. Actually, you have already taught the precursor to this trick in a previous chapter, stretching. You will now add those elements to this grand pose. It is best not to begin teaching this trick to a horse on grass, as it will only serve as a distraction. The cues for this trick are quite different than for any other movements.

STEP 1: Outfit your horse in a bridle. Stand him in a stall, aisle or fence, with his right side next to the wall. The saddle and pad may be on or off the horse. Standing on the left side of the horse, with the reins in your left hand and the whip in your right, cue the horse to start a stretching position, lifting the horse's head up a little. The horse's front feet should step forward about a foot. Reward him with a carrot and make a fuss over him.

STEP 2: Repeat Step 1. Now you are ready to ask the horse to bring his body down and back. With the reins in your left hand, take a carrot, show it to the horse, and bring the carrot down a little, close to the horse's knees, and feed it to him there. Repeat this several times, to bring the

Photo courtesy of Chris Sartre

horse's head down. Be satisfied with a little movement in the right direction. If the horse should move his front feet back, you will need to ask him to stretch them out again. If he steps back with his hind feet, that would be fine.

STEP 3: Repeat Steps 1 and 2. Take the carrot this time and put it even further down between the horse's legs, closer to the ground, making him reach for it, bringing his body down and his back up, telling him to "CURTSY!" Feed him the carrot there. Repeat this several times.

STEP 4: Repeat Steps 1, 2 and 3. This time, as you feed your horse the carrot low to the ground, giving him the command to "CURTSY!", tap him behind his left elbow on the girth area with the whip, under his barrel. Repeat several times.

STEP 5: Repeat Step 4, eliminating the carrot, and just using the whip. After he has done the curtsy, reward him with a carrot.

Note: Space the above steps in intervals, making each step a session. Some horses will go very low in the CURTSY BOW, and others have difficulty going as low. Try not to do this movement on slippery surfaces, since the horse's front feet will have little weight on them as they stretch out, and if the horse feels like he will slip, he will be reluctant to do this movement.

From the saddle: At first you may put just about anyone in the saddle and you can cue your horse for the circus bow from the ground. Once you have started the curtsy bow from the saddle, you may find it easier to give the cue with the whip held in the right hand and tap behind the elbow on the right side. The whip, if used low on the horse, will touch his barrel and act on both sides. Raise your left hand to present your performing trick horse to the audience, and expect lots of cheers and applause! Give him lots of pats and praise.

Variation:

A very grandiose movement is to have the horse cross his legs, as in the trick ACTING DRUNK, and then cue him for the curtsy bow. This is really impressive!

Photo courtesy of Cynthia McFarland

PEDESTAL POSE:
Statue of Liberty

Equipment needed: bridle, saddle and saddle pad (when mounted), whip, pedestal, carrots.

Once you have taught your horse the tricks of SHAKING HANDS and COUNTING, you may then teach him the pedestal mount. Be sure your pedestal is well-built, safe, non-slippery, and is capable of holding the weight of your horse and a rider (see Appendix for pedestal construction). Make certain it is sturdy enough so the horse can't knock it over as he goes to mount by putting his front feet on the edge of the pedestal. If the horse should have his feet slip off he may be frightened and afraid to try mounting again. The pedestal should be light enough so that it can be moved from place to place yet sturdy enough so that it won't turn over or he won't slip off.

The pedestal mount is first taught with the horse's forefeet, then all four feet (END OF THE TRAIL POSE), and last the hind feet only on the pedestal. We will begin with the horse's front feet on the pedestal, then proceed to have one forefoot on the pedestal and the other raised in the air on a perch, resembling the pose of the STATUE OF LIBERTY.

It helps to have taught the horse to walk over a wooden "bridge" before teaching this trick so he is accustomed to the sound of wood under his

Ta-da!
Photo courtesy of Chris Sartre

64

feet and a wooden surface. The ideal place to teach this trick is in a ring, about a couple of feet from each wall in the corner.

STEP 1: Have a bridle on your horse, and with the reins in your left hand close to the bit, and the whip in your right hand, lead the horse up to the pedestal and let him look and smell it as you pet and reassure him. When the horse is standing about a foot from the pedestal with both front feet, tap the horse on the left shoulder with the whip, telling him, "LIFT," until he makes an attempt to mount with the left foot. Stroke his legs reassuringly as you talk to him in a soothing tone of voice. At first, he may have some trouble finding the pedestal and putting his foot on it. As soon as his left foot finds the pedestal, move the horse forward with your left hand leading the horse forward, so that he puts weight on that foot that is on the pedestal. Don't be discour-

aged if he paws or misses the pedestal at first. If he stands quietly about a foot away from it, pick his left foot up and place it on the pedestal, even if he bends it and doesn't put any weight on it. When you move him forward by pulling gently on the reins and using the whip on his rump or on his hind legs, he will step forward with the hind legs and put weight on the left leg which is on the pedestal. He will then put his right foot up, and you should immediately reward him with a carrot and make a huge fuss. Let him stand there for a moment, and then lead him off. If he should mount the pedestal by himself, be sure to take him off immediately. The horse should under no circumstance try and mount the pedestal until you ask him to. Put the horse away for a while before returning to attempt it again.

STEP 2: Repeat Step 1 until your horse has mastered putting his front feet

up on the pedestal. Move slightly in front of him and cue your horse to shake hands with his right foreleg, tapping him on the right ankle with the whip, asking him for an extension of that leg. Reward him for any correct movement. Let him stand there a moment and lead him off the pedestal and repeat this several more times.

STEP 3: Repeat Steps 1 and 2. Now that he will extend his right foreleg while standing with the left foreleg on the pedestal, take hold of the right foot and place it on the perch. Reward him while he hold it there a few seconds, keeping the whip on his right ankle and telling him "whoa."

STEP 4: Repeat Step 3, asking your horse to hold his right foot up on the perch for longer periods of time. His cue to remove his foot from the perch is when you take the whip off his foot. Raise your hand up in the

air to present this trick in a grandiose way, as if to say, "Ta-da!"

From the saddle: You will need a ground person to help with this at first. As your ground person gives the cues for your horse to mount the pedestal with you mounted in the saddle, take a long buggy whip in your right hand, and as your ground person cues the horse by tapping on his right ankle, you can simultaneously cue the horse, by

reaching over and tapping him on the right foreleg. Pretty soon, you will be able to cue your horse to do this without the help of the ground person.

When your horse masters this trick, he qualifies as an exceptional trick horse!

Other Variations?

I leave these to your own fertile imagination!

I pledge allegiance...
Photo courtesy of Michelle Younghans

65

END OF THE TRAIL POSE: Pedestal Pose with All Four Feet

Equipment needed: bridle, saddle and saddle pad
(if mounted), whip, carrots.

This trick is where you can shine as an exceptional trainer. This trick will take some time, but it's worth every minute. In the beginning of teaching the pedestal mount with all four feet, you may need to have a larger pedestal, one with a diameter of at least 2 feet. Having this constructed in the manner specified (see Appendix) will cost some money, but if you have spent this much time   and effort on your horse, you can't fail him now! Also, at this point, you have an accomplished horse, your tricks are a little more spectacular, your cues more refined.   If you are training a horse, train him to his full potential! Take all pains necessary to prevent him from getting hurt.

STEP 1: Outfitted with the bridle, saddle pad and saddle, have the horse mount the pedestal with both front feet as in the previous trick, the STATUE OF LIBERTY, having the pedestal moved farther from the wall. Do not ask the horse to extend his right front leg, however. Reward him with a carrot.

STEP 2: Repeat Step 1. When both front feet are on the pedestal, you will act on the hind legs to move them forward more under his body, tapping on the hind legs below the hocks with the whip in your right hand, to get

Photo courtesy of Chris Sartre

them closer to the pedestal. Take your time, reward the horse with a carrot and reassure him.

STEP 3: Repeat Steps 1 and 2. As soon as the horse's hind legs are near the pedestal that the front feet are on, run your hand down his left hind leg, asking him to "LIFT" the leg off the ground. When it is off the ground, take the left foot and place it on the pedestal. Let him stand with just three feet on the pedestal and reward him with a carrot. Repeat a few times and end the session.

STEP 4: Repeat Steps 1, 2 and 3. Take your time in asking the horse to put his hind feet on the pedestal, because he has to learn to balance himself in a new position. As you did with the left leg, ask the horse to move the right hind foot on the pedestal, switching to the right side of the horse, if necessary to cue

him, until all four feet are on the pedestal. Reward him generously, and reassure him. Hold him there for a few seconds. To dismount from the pedestal, the horse should always come off with the front feet first. This should be done slowly, with the hind feet last to come off the pedestal. Gradually increase the amount of time before you have the horse dismount from the pedestal, and ask him to lower his head by pulling down gently on the reins, holding his head in position. Now your horse looks like the famous portrait, the "END OF THE TRAIL."

Note: You will need to position your horse's front feet forward on the pedestal so that he has room to place all four feet. Try and hold the reins firmly so that a front foot doesn't move off the pedestal. Proceed with the utmost patience in teaching this trick, and you will have hit the jackpot.

From the saddle: Use a ground person while you are mounted in the saddle, and have him give the cues from the ground as you did before to raise his hind legs. You will then practice with your whip tapping the horse's left hind foot and then his right hind leg. Take it slowly, and he will find his balance with your weight in the saddle. Reward him generously, and practice him standing on the pedestal for increased amounts of time. Raise your hand and wave to the cheers and applause of your audience. 🐴

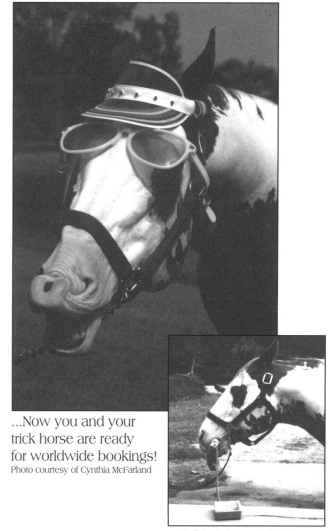

...Now you and your trick horse are ready for worldwide bookings!
Photo courtesy of Cynthia McFarland

Quick! Get my agent on the line.
Photo courtesy of Michelle Younghans

Pedestal

The equipment shown at right is the equipment you will want to have built for your pedestal. The dimensions are 18" high; base spread of 3' apart; top (pedestal stand) is 24" square.

It should be constructed out of 5/8 inch plywood and reinforced with 2" x 4" wood studs. This is adequate for a horse up to 1250 lbs. If you have a smaller horse, pony or miniature horse, you should adjust the construction for them.

The top has either carpet or rubber on it so that it is not slippery for the horse. This material is fastened down.

Important Note: When attempting to make this pedestal and the perch on page 70, work with or hire someone who is *very* knowledgeable about wood construction. Your platform needs to be sturdy enough and safe enough to hold a 1200 lb horse. Do not take any short cuts — money-wise or construction-wise — when building this platform. And also do not attempt to stand your horse on *anything* that would not adequately hold his weight, might tip over or even injure him.

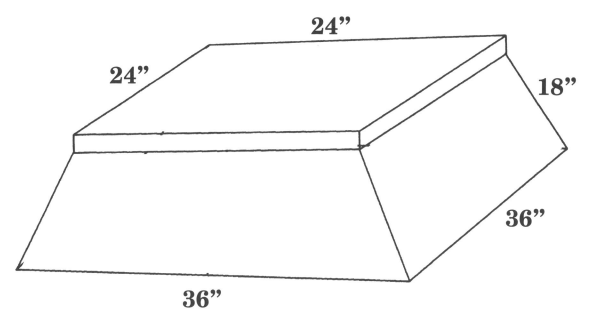

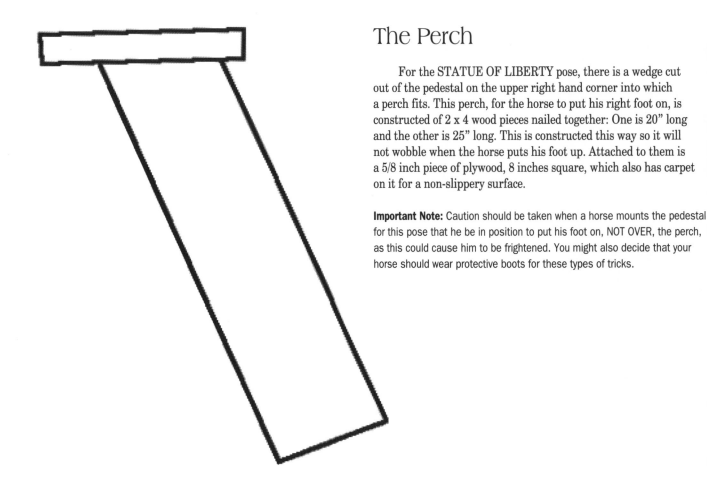

The Perch

For the STATUE OF LIBERTY pose, there is a wedge cut out of the pedestal on the upper right hand corner into which a perch fits. This perch, for the horse to put his right foot on, is constructed of 2 x 4 wood pieces nailed together: One is 20" long and the other is 25" long. This is constructed this way so it will not wobble when the horse puts his foot up. Attached to them is a 5/8 inch piece of plywood, 8 inches square, which also has carpet on it for a non-slippery surface.

Important Note: Caution should be taken when a horse mounts the pedestal for this pose that he be in position to put his foot on, NOT OVER, the perch, as this could cause him to be frightened. You might also decide that your horse should wear protective boots for these types of tricks.

CURTAIN CALL

Photo courtesy of Chris Sartre

N ow that you and your horse have graduated (you NEVER really graduate, because he never completes his full potential in learning), you have earned a well-deserved pat on the back. You have found out that the more your horse learns—the more he is capable of learning.

Share your patience with your horse and your horse will show you how good a horse trainer you are. Keep reminding yourself: May I always be the kind of person my horse thinks I am. It is a joy and a real treat to see a horse trained to perfection through patience and reward. Remember—love and patience are the methods and the rewards.

Be firm but gentle. Always be on guard for the safety of your horse, no matter where you perform. Make sure you take your time and analyze what you and your horse are doing. Begin at the beginning, taking no shortcuts, in order to produce the correctly trained horse. Be an artist in your training and pay attention to the details.

I hope this book provides you with the know-how so that you can enjoy training your trick horse as much as I do.

Now that you've caught me in my act,
I hope to catch yours one day!

Write Us!

❤ Be included in our other books! Do you have any recipes, grooming tips, remedies, horse costumes, unique tricks you've taught your horse, or just comments you'd like to share? E-mail us or drop us a note at the addresses below.

❤ Mail us any funny, cute, unusual pictures of your horse that we can use in upcoming books and newsletters.

❤ Look for other Horse Hollow Press books at your local tack store: *The Original Book of Horse Treats* (a cook book of treats and things you can make for your horse); *The Ultimate Guide to Pampering Your Horse* (a guide to pampering tips and handy hints); *The Incredible Little Book of 10,001 Names for Horses* (a listing of literally thousands of names) and *Horse Lover's Birthday Book* (a book of days to remember and a guide for gifts for horses, *and humans,* that you can make yourself.)

❤ Watch for Carole Fletcher's second book, *Advanced Trickonometry*, published by Horse Hollow Press.

❤ Want to drop a note directly to the author? Write to: Carole Fletcher, Singin' Saddles Ranch, 8100 NW 120th St., Reddick, FL 32686 or e-mail her at: trickhorse@worldnet.att.net or visit her web site: www.trickhorse.com for more books and videos by Carole Fletcher.

❤ For a free catalog of horse books, write us at Horse Hollow Press or visit our web site: www.horsehollowpress.com

HORSE HOLLOW PRESS, Inc.
P.O. Box 456, Goshen, NY 10924-0456
www.horsehollowpress.com
e-mail: info@horsehollowpress.com

72

Order more copies!

VISIT YOUR FAVORITE TACK & FEED OR BOOK STORE!

Yes! I want to order more books. Please send me:

QTY:

____ *Trickonometry: The Secrets of Teaching Your Horse Tricks*. $23.95

____ *The Original Book of Horse Treats*. $19.95 • Cookbook of horse treats.

____ *Anyone Can Draw Horses*. $7.95 • Like the title says, teaches *anyone* to draw horses!

____ *The Ultimate Guide to Pampering Your Horse*. $24.95 Hundreds of pampering tips and handy hints to please your horse.

____ *The Incredible Little Book of 10,001 Names for Horses*. $8.95 Literally thousands of names for horses and ponies.

____ *Horse Lover's Birthday Book*. Paperback. $4.95 • A book of days to remember as well as a guide to gifts for horses and humans you can make yourself.

Add $4.95 for shipping & handling per order. Pay only one price for shipping, no additional needed for more books ordered. **TOTAL ENCLOSED: $_____**
(If you are ordering only the *Horse Lover's Birthday Book*, only include $1.00 for shipping and handling.)
(Check, money order, or credit cards accepted. NY residents, please add sales tax.)

OR CALL TOLL-FREE: 1-800-4-1-HORSE to order!

Name: _____

Address: _____

City/State/Zip: _____

Phone: _____

Visa/MC/AMEX: _____ Exp. Date: _____

Signature: _____